Every endeavor is directly rel[illegible] d over a lifetime. In this new ve[illegible] *Heart of the Artist*, Rory Noland reveals a pathway essential for Christian artists to experience successful ministries. Skill is included in the development of an artist, but character and a willingness to obey Christ is the foundational requirement. Every Christian artist needs the content of this work to guide them on this amazing journey.

—Stan Endicott, Chief Culture Office, Slingshot Group

This book not only was highly influential in my own ministry and leadership journey but also is a resource I have used time and again in the development and formation of young leaders. This second edition with new content is a godsend for today's generation of creatives and creative leaders. Rory will continue to save artists who read this from unnecessary landmines and help them walk more fully in God's plan and purpose for their lives and gifting. Whether or not you've read it before, it's a must-read!

—Tim Foot, Vice President of Senior Leadership and Experience, Slingshot Group

This book is simply one of the greatest tools you can put in your tool belt as a worship leader or creative in the church. Whether you've been in ministry for twenty days or twenty years, it will challenge you toward godly character and leadership development and provide you with practical insights for stewarding your creative heart as well as the hearts of the creatives you have been entrusted to lead.

—Kyle Fredricks, Worship Pastor, Harvest Church, North Indianapolis

As worship leaders, it is incredibly important to create a culture of integrity and authenticity on our teams. Reading this book with my team really broke the ice for us to honestly talk about struggling with sin as creatives in the church. It's a tool that I will come back to again and again.

—Zach Jones, Director of Worship, Flatland Church, Omaha, NE

I took my team through this book, and I will never forget our discussions on what we had read and how it began to shape us. But I never expected it to grow a healthy team of worshipers like it did. This book caused ministry to flourish simply because we chose to be worshiping artists and not performers. It weeded out that mindset. This is the one tool that I can definitely say empowered authentic worship.

—Lee Lukazewski, Adult Ministries Pastor, Christ Community Church

This book heavily influenced me in a critical time in my life. I was wrestling with my role as a worship leader in a megachurch, looking for answers to many questions. Rory seemed to know what was happening inside my heart and head and provided the answers. Better yet, he pointed me to where to find the answers: Scripture. After I soaked up the content, I used it as a framework for Bible study and discipleship with my team members. Later I was blessed to start a nonprofit organization dedicated to serving artists of all walks of life. I highly recommend this book and look forward to the next generation being exposed to its biblical truth, historical facts, and practical tools for living and serving as a Christian creative.

—Ben Shafer, Executive Director, 402 Arts Collective

Twenty-one years ago, I read the first edition of this book. At that time, it impacted, influenced and shaped our worship ministry in profound ways. Worship pastors everywhere are now rejoicing that we have a second edition. I commend Rory for addressing the challenging character issues we all deal with. His real-life illustrations, his connecting us to Scripture, and his discussion questions and action steps make this one of the most comprehensive worship resources anywhere. This new edition is as important now as his original was twenty-one years ago—maybe more.

—Dennis Worley, Lead Worship Minister, Brentwood Baptist Church, Brentwood, TN

THE HEART OF THE ARTIST

SECOND EDITION

THE HEART OF THE ARTIST

A CHARACTER-BUILDING GUIDE FOR YOU AND YOUR MINISTRY TEAM

SECOND EDITION

RORY NOLAND

ZONDERVAN REFLECTIVE

ZONDERVAN REFLECTIVE

The Heart of the Artist, Second Edition

Published in Grand Rapids, Michigan, by Zondervan. Zondervan is a registered trademark of The Zondervan Corporation, L.L.C., a wholly owned subsidiary of HarperCollins Christian Publishing, Inc.

Requests for information should be addressed to customercare@harpercollins.com.

Zondervan titles may be purchased in bulk for educational, business, fundraising, or sales promotional use. For information, please email SpecialMarkets@Zondervan .com.

ISBN 978-0-310-11170-2 (softcover)
ISBN 978-0-310-12021-6 (audio)
ISBN 978-0-310-11171-9 (ebook)

Cover Design: Micah Kandros Design
Cover Art: © Alexander Evgenvevich / Shutterstock
Interior Design: Denise Froehlich

Printed in the United States of America

24 25 26 27 28 LBC 7 6 5 4 3

CONTENTS

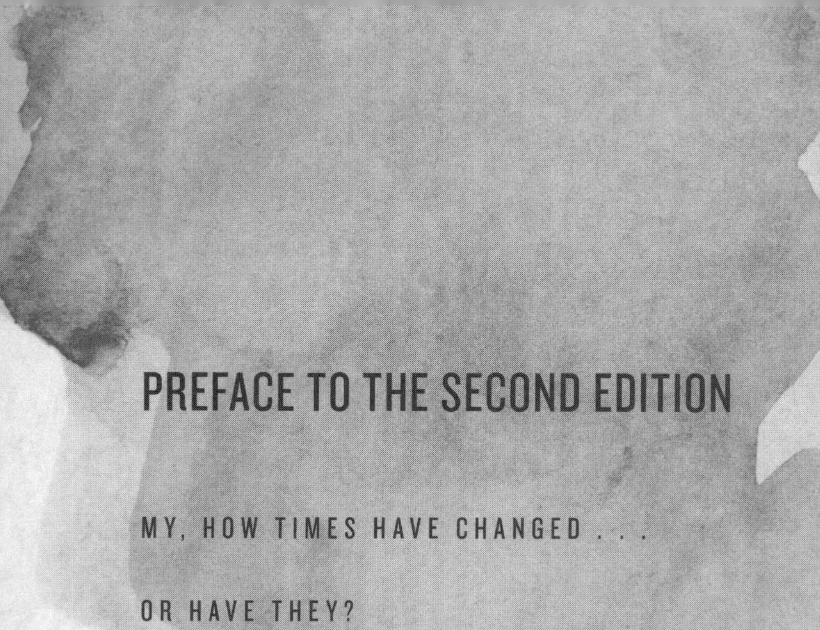

PREFACE TO THE SECOND EDITION

MY, HOW TIMES HAVE CHANGED . . . OR HAVE THEY?

I HAVE SEEN A LOT OF changes in the forty-plus years I've been involved in worship ministry. It was called "music ministry" when I started out in church work. My first job title was Music Director; at another church my business card read Minister of Music. My main responsibility in those settings was to prepare "special music" for a variety of vocal ensembles to sing at Sunday services. I was the "contemporary music" guy. In the early 1970s, contemporary Christian music was just emerging as an up-and-coming force in the recording industry. My church was among a small number of congregations that were incorporating songs into our Sunday services from favorite Christian rock bands like Love Song, Second Chapter of Acts, the Imperials, and the

Archers. Songs by Amy Grant, Andrae Crouch, and later Sandi Patty, Larnelle Harris, and Steve Green gave our more capable soloists material they could sink their teeth into. In those days we couldn't download charts and upload them to Planning Center. We transcribed each song, so we had to listen to it over and over, figure out the chords and the vocal parts, and then write it all down by hand. We had to call our volunteers on the phone to ask them to sing or play every weekend.

Character Still Matters

My little jaunt down memory lane is not meant to infer that things were so much better back in the day. I assure you, I'm not one of those old guys who thinks that worship ministry was so much better in my day. On the contrary, there is so much great praise music being written these days. The quality of musicianship in our churches keeps rising. Young worship leaders today are passionate about the Lord.

Worship ministry has changed a lot over the past four decades and mostly for the better. However, I can't help but notice that the more things change, the more one thing remains the same—we artists in the church still need to model Christian character. Godly character matters as much today as it did forty years ago.

I repeatedly tell church artists that being involved in

worship ministry can be the ultimate character-building experience; it certainly forced me to grow up in a hurry and still demands that I deal with my personal issues. Whether we're on staff at a church or simply volunteering, interacting regularly with church people eventually exposes our dysfunctional behavior patterns, emotional baggage, and blind spots. Ministering alongside other artists can force us to confront our fears, insecurities, and selfish motives. Church work is downright hazardous to the spiritual status quo, for it continually challenges us to stay attentive to our ongoing character development.

I'm embarrassed to admit how spiritually immature I was in my early days of ministry. Whenever conflict occurred, I was convinced it was everyone else's fault. Certainly not mine! Much to my surprise, I began noticing that more often than not I was to blame; I was the cause of the strife. Or at the very least my stuff was exacerbating the problem. My immaturity and lack of character threatened to undermine the ministry I was trying to build.

For starters, I was prideful, overly sensitive, and defensive. I could be stubborn, willful, and self-centered. I struggled with jealousy and envy. I was crippled by perfectionism, and I had deep insecurity issues. And that was me on a good day!

I didn't write *The Heart of the Artist* because I had life all figured out and had conquered all my shortcomings. I have struggled with every character defect discussed in this book, and I continue to wrestle with my old nature. I have learned much along the way, most of which grew out of my quiet times with the Lord. I'm happy to report that I have made significant progress over the years. The Lord, in his mercy, has grown me up in significant ways, but I certainly haven't arrived yet. I continue to apply the things I share in these pages, and I feel privileged to be able to pass on what I've learned to the next generation of church artists.

What's New in This Second Edition?

This second edition contains a great deal of new content. As I've taught this material over the years, I've continued to add new insights and illustrations. While this edition contains the same basic content as the original, it reflects additional learning I've gained since the book's first publication. I've updated the scenarios at the beginning of each chapter that, along with the discussion questions, introduce the chapter's topic. People often ask me whether these short, slice-of-church-life stories are true. I assure them they are; each one is based on real people I've known or encountered while ministering in the church. But I jokingly add that the names have been changed to protect the guilty. This updated version also benefits from the fact that I am a better writer now. I was quite wordy in my younger days. Hopefully, readers will find this edition more focused and streamlined.

How to Use This Book

The Heart of the Artist can be used effectively for personal or small group study. I hear from pastors who use it as a discipleship tool for their worship leaders. I know worship leaders who make it mandatory reading for their volunteers, choir directors who take their choir members through it, and tech directors who buy copies for each team member. I'm also aware of college professors who use the book in the classroom. For group study, I highly recommend incorporating the book's discussion questions, especially the ones at the end of each chapter. Those follow-up questions enable readers to wrestle with the content presented in that chapter and consider how to apply it. Hearing what someone else got out of the reading challenges everyone in the group to identify a takeaway for themselves.

Honoring God with Your Talent and Your Life

When the first edition of this book was first released, I claimed enthusiastically that we were on the verge of a golden era for the arts in the church, which seemed like a bold statement at the time. Two decades later, that no longer sounds like such a far-fetched idea. The arts play an increasingly vital role in worship today, as do artists. As I travel, I see artists all over the world discovering the joy and reward that come from using their talents to serve the Lord. More than ever, I am convinced that God is raising up a global community of artists who are fully devoted to the lordship of Jesus Christ in their lives. As I did twenty years ago, I challenge the artists of today to take stock spiritually and make sure they are honoring God not only with their gifts but also with their lives. Let's continue to be as serious about developing godly character as we are about honing our talent. Let's be artists who are known not only for their talent but also for their walk with Christ.

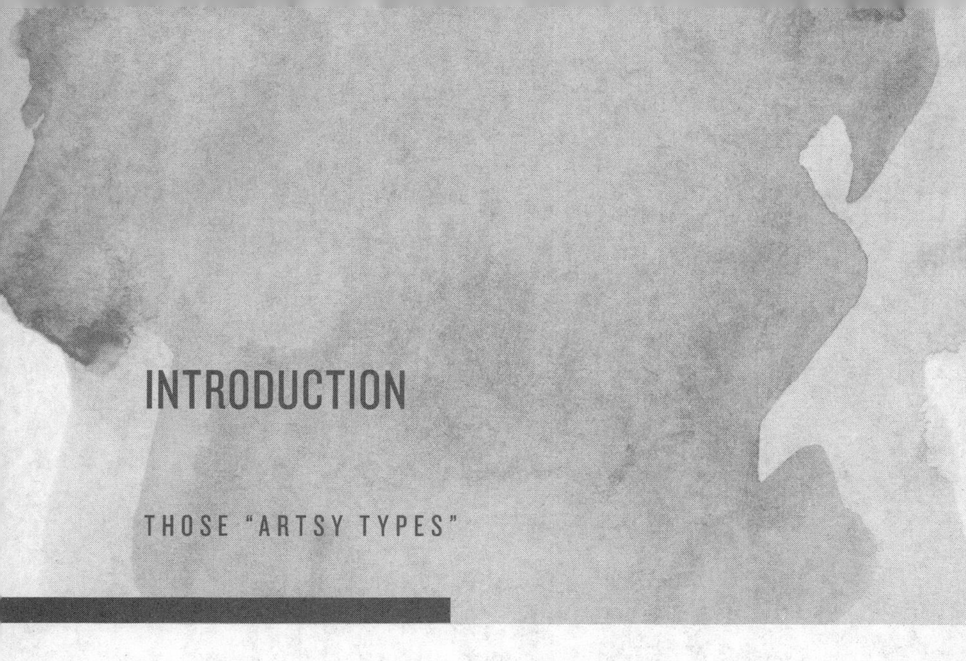

INTRODUCTION

THOSE "ARTSY TYPES"

I REMEMBER SPEAKING AT A CONFERENCE in Fort Lauderdale years ago that was attended mostly by pastors and church leaders. I was asked to speak about the state of church music and the future of the arts in the church. However, my deeper passion is for Christian artists to live with integrity and godly character, so I sneaked in a few words on that topic. Though I hardly mentioned it, there was a flurry of questions afterward, all dealing with the character and integrity of artists in the church.

To this day, the majority of the questions I get about music ministry have little to do with music. They revolve around character issues.

- How can I get my volunteers to understand what it means to have a servant's heart?

- How can I cultivate unity on the team?
- How can I get my musicians to get along with each other?
- What should I do about the attitude problems pervading the ranks?
- How can I help those struggling with perfectionism, criticism, envy, or temptation?
- What style of leadership works best with artists?

The worship department and other arts-related ministries seem to be a hotbed for serious character problems. I've seen more than a few worship ministries torn apart because their leaders failed to address such issues in themselves as well as in those they lead. I typically see churches handle their artists in one of two ways. We either coddle them and put up with their shortcomings, or we use and abuse them.

I've had pastors call me, frustrated over character issues with their worship staff. "Our worship leader doesn't listen to suggestions," they'll say. Or, "He doesn't take criticism well. He's not a team player. He's more interested in doing his own thing."

I've also heard creative arts pastors express similar frustrations about their volunteers. "So-and-so is a great guitar player, but they're just so difficult to work with." Or, "Our key vocalist throws a temper tantrum and threatens to quit once a month. We don't know what to do, because we can't afford to lose our best singer right now." For too long churches have ignored the problem, letting artists' character slide. But looking the other way or hoping the problem goes away by itself only makes matters worse.

Irving Stone's *The Agony and the Ecstasy*, a biographical novel about the life of Michelangelo, has one long chapter devoted to the artist's relationships with the various popes he worked for. Most of those relationships were stormy ones, and Michelangelo's experience as a church artist was extremely frustrating. As I read about all the abuse heaped upon one of my favorite artists, the thought occurred to me that this tension between the church and artists has been going on for hundreds of years. I dream of the day when the church stops alienating artists and starts nurturing them. I long for the church to be a safe place for artists, a place where they can grow and become the people God created them to be.

About the Term *Artist*

When I use the word artist, I cast a wide net to include anyone and everyone who does anything artistic. I'm referring to those who perform, write, create, or produce art, which includes musicians, dancers, actors, writers, poets, painters, visual artists, performers, producers, photographers. It also includes those who work in technical areas such as sound, lighting, video, film, staging, as well as computer graphics and design. Even if you have never referred to yourself as an artist, if you do artistic things, chances are you have some kind of artistic streak, large or small or somewhere in between.

You might be trying to pursue a career in the arts or dabbling in the arts as a hobby. Maybe the extent of your artistic involvement is that you sing in the back row of the church choir. You could be an amateur or a professional. You might be a performer, an essence creator, or both. Perhaps you work with artists or live with an artist and want to understand them better. Whatever the case, being any kind of artist comes with certain challenges, especially for those who serve in the church.

The Artistic Temperament

If you engage in artistic endeavor, you also have, to varying degrees, the temperament that goes along with being a musician or an artist. No other temperament known to humankind is both celebrated and maligned as much as the artistic temperament. If you're an artist, chances are pretty good that at some point in your life, you've been made to feel like you're different. Maybe even strange or weird. Perhaps you feel like you don't fit in anywhere or that nobody gets you.

After that conference in Fort Lauderdale, a pastor sat with me on the shuttle bus back to the hotel because he wanted my advice about working with artists. He began the conversation by admitting that he was at a loss as to how to relate to the artists serving at his church. "I just leave those artsy types alone," he said. "They're kinda off in their own little world anyway." What did he mean by "those artsy types"? And why did he make being an artist sound so creepy?

Unfortunately, certain negative stereotypes are attached to people with the artistic temperament. Some people say that we are temperamental and eccentric. Some people think we are difficult, moody, and emotionally unstable. Others see us as free-spirited, quirky, and undisciplined. Excuses are often made for our shortcomings, more so than for those of any other temperament. The problem occurs when we artists buy into those excuses and use them to justify unacceptable behavior.

I remember my son informing me that in school he was learning about how weird musicians are. He was taking a music appreciation class, and what stood out to him was that Beethoven had such a bad temper that he would cause a scene in a restaurant if his food wasn't right, that women would throw their room keys onstage at Franz Liszt, and that Wagner was a quirky man with strong anti-Semitic views. Since so many of the musicians he was learning about were bizarre eccentrics, it made me wonder what he thought about me!

For centuries scholars have been fascinated with the artistic temperament. It started with the ancient Greeks, who divided human personality into four main categories: choleric, sanguine, phlegmatic, and melancholy. These four classifications, which factored into the development of modern psychology, represent our predisposition to life, our innate tendencies. Think of your temperament as the way you're wired. It's your natural way of being in the world.

Aristotle said that "all extraordinary men distinguished in philosophy, politics, poetry, and the arts are evidently melancholic."[1] As a result, the artistic temperament became associated with melancholia. People with an artistic bent were labeled melancholy, which is misleading because not all artists have melancholic tendencies.

In the Middle Ages, melancholy was considered a physical disorder, and the church regarded it as a sin similar to slothfulness.[2] But during the Renaissance, melancholy came to be seen as a divine gift. Influenced by astrology, many believed a person's behavior was determined at birth by his or her planet's conjunction with other celestial bodies. Within this framework, Saturn was associated with melancholy. Someone born under Saturn would "be either sane and capable of rare accomplishment or sick and condemned to inertia and stupidity."[3] The capability for rare accomplishment obviously made the melancholy temperament quite fashionable during the Renaissance. It was written that "a veritable wave of 'melancholic behavior' swept across Europe" during the sixteenth century.[4] The more eccentric an artist was, the more he or she was considered a genius.

In spite of this rather exalted view, which continued well into the Romantic period, the melancholy temperament has always had its share of negative press. Even at a time when it was in vogue, some were expressing concern about those who exhibited melancholic tendencies. Writing in the year 1586 (and in the style of that day), physician Timothy Bright described the melancholy person as

> cold and dry; of color black and swart; of substance inclining to hardness; lean and sparse of flesh . . . of memory reasonably good if fancies deface it not; firm in opinion, and hardly removed where it is resolved; doubtful before, and long in deliberation; suspicious, painful in studies, and circumspect; given to fearful and terrible dreams; in affection sad and full of fear, hardly moved to anger but keeping it long, and not easy to be reconciled; envious and jealous, apt to take occasions in the worst part, and out of measure passionate. From these two dispositions of brain and heart arise solitariness, mourning, weeping . . . sighing, sobbing, lamentation, countenance demise and hanging down, blushing and bashful; of pace slow, silent, negligent, refusing the light and frequency of men, delighted more in solitariness and obscurity.[5]

Not a very flattering picture, is it? Even today there's a certain stigma attached to the melancholy temperament. Most studies of the temperaments present the melancholy type with a great deal of ambivalence. The other three temperaments come off smelling like a rose, while the dreaded melancholy temperament sounds so awful. At least that's how it seems to me. Because melancholia is associated with artists, we are often seen as analytical to a fault, moody, unsociable, and overly sensitive. What bothers me most is that if you get labeled a melancholic or even an artist, it is assumed that you are some maladjusted emotional misfit.

My artistic friend, I assure you that there is nothing wrong with you. You are not a misfit. You're an artist! That's what God created you to be. He doesn't look at you as one of those strange artsy types. Your heavenly Father loves you and understands you. Your vibrant creativity is a gift from an infinitely creative God. Your fire and passion are a reflection of God's heart for what is good and right. Your quest for beauty is inherited from the one who fills the universe with breathtaking splendor. I celebrate the artist in each and every one of you.

Reclaiming the Artistic Temperament for Christ

I believe that God has redeemed the artistic temperament. If you're in Christ, you are a new creature. "The old has gone, the new is here!" (2 Cor. 5:17). So bring on the new you in Christ—that beautiful, fully alive, Spirit-filled artist God created you to be.

I'll admit we are a little different, but I'm convinced it's a good kind of different. Artists look at things differently than nonartists do. We notice detail; we appreciate nuance and beauty. Some people might look at the evening sky and see only a bunch of stars. But an artist looks at it and sees beauty and meaning. Artists want to sit under the stars and soak in all their grandeur. They want to gaze at the moon and be dazzled. They want to paint a picture of it or write a song or a poem. Debussy was so moved by the evening sky that he wrote *Clair de Lune*. Van Gogh was inspired and painted *Starry Night*. King David looked at the evening sky and wrote a praise song:

> When I consider your heavens,
> the work of your fingers,
> the moon and the stars,
> which you have set in place,
> what is mankind that you are mindful of them,
> human beings that you care for them?
>
> —PSALM 8:3–4

Artists respond differently to things than nonartists do. We tend to be more sensitive. And that's okay. That's how God made us. In Ephesians, Paul talks about having the eyes of our hearts enlightened (1:18). Sensitive people have a lot of heart. We might see things differently because we feel deeply. In *Windows of the Soul*, Ken Gire writes, "We learn from the artists, from those who work in paint or words, or musical notes, from those who have eyes that see and ears that hear and hearts that feel deeply and passionately about all that is sacred and dear to God."[6]

For this reason, artists often speak out against injustice, inequality, and hypocrisy. They take up the cause of those who are suffering. They make us more sensitive to the lost and lonely and to the plight of the downtrodden. Have you ever been moved to tears by a powerful piece of music or held spellbound by a beautiful work of art? Have you ever been moved by a scene from a film? It's because an artist communicated his or her feelings in such a powerful way that it touched your heart and soul.

The Arts in the Bible

Let's examine briefly what the Bible has to say about the arts and artists. Along with being the infallible Word of God and an agent of change, the Bible itself is a work of art. People throughout history have studied it as an example of exquisite literature. One such scholar was Frank E. Gaebelein, who wrote, "It is a fact that over and above any other piece of world literature from Homer down through Virgil, Dante, Cervantes, Shakespeare, Milton, and Goethe, no book has been more fully acknowledged as great simply as a book than the Bible."[7]

The Bible is rich in its artistic use of metaphor. My favorite example is the last chapter of Ecclesiastes, in which the aging process is treated metaphorically and likened to a house. "When the keepers of the house tremble, and the strong men stoop, when the grinders cease because they are few, and those looking through the windows grow dim; when the doors to the street are closed and the sound of grinding fades; when people rise up at the sound of birds, but all their songs grow faint" (12:3–4).

The trembling "keepers of the house" refers to hands that shake when one grows old. The "grinders" refer to teeth and our propensity to lose them as we age. Losing our eyesight is described as looking through a window and having the image grow dimmer. Other references to being bent over, losing one's hearing, and having insomnia are all included in this clever analogy. Instead of describing the aging process in clinical terms, the writer appeals to our imagination and in so doing gets us to feel a sadness about growing old.

The Bible also contains poetry that is written with a great deal of skill and sophistication. The Psalms, the book of Job, and Song of Songs are prominent examples of biblical poetry.

Drama is first mentioned in the Bible when Ezekiel is instructed to act out a brief play depicting the siege of Jerusalem.

He even drew the city skyline and used it as a familiar backdrop (Ezekiel 4). Jesus spoke often in parables and told colorful and intriguing stories that had their share of drama to them.

The visual arts played a major role in building the tabernacle (Ex. 31:1–11). Francis Schaeffer points out that the tabernacle involved every form of representational art known to man.[8] The visual arts were a major factor in the decor of the temple. The temple was decked out with the finest carvings and engravings (1 Kings 6:15–36; 7:23–39; 2 Chron. 3:5–7; 4:1–7). First Kings 6:4 says that Solomon "made windows with artistic frames" (NASB). Some of the artwork in the temple, like the ornately decorated freestanding columns, had no utilitarian significance but exemplified beauty for its own sake (2 Chron. 3:15–17).

Music is also mentioned quite often in the Bible. Singing was a big part of ancient Hebrew culture. The book of Psalms is actually a hymnbook, and it continually exhorts us to sing to the Lord (Ps. 149:1). The nation of Israel not only sang during worship, they sang while they worked (Num. 21:16–18). David sang a song he wrote at the deaths of Saul and Jonathan (2 Sam. 1:19–27). And as you leaf through the pages of the book of Revelation, it's obvious that we'll be doing a lot of singing in heaven (19:1–8).

There is also plenty of instrumental music in the Bible. The word *selah*, which occurs throughout the Psalms (seventy-one times, to be exact), is most likely referring to an instrumental interlude between verses or sections of vocal music. Trumpets were used to summon the nation of Israel for meetings, as a signal to break camp, in feasts, in commemorations, during worship, and in conjunction with various military campaigns (Lev. 23:24; Num. 10:1–10; 29:1; Josh. 6:20; Judg. 3:27; 6:34; 7:19–22; 1 Sam. 13:3; 2 Sam. 2:28; 15:10; 18:16; 1 Kings 1:34; 2 Kings 9:13; Ps. 150:3). Trumpets will also announce the second coming of Christ and the resurrection of the dead (Matt. 24:31; 1 Cor. 15:52). Other instruments mentioned include the flute, lyre, harp, and various percussion instruments (1 Sam. 10:5; 1 Kings 1:40; 1 Chron. 25:1; Pss. 45:8; 92:1–3, 150:3–5; Matt. 9:23).

Dance is sanctioned in the Bible. Psalm 149:3 says, "Let them praise his name with dancing." Psalm 150:4 also says, "Praise him with timbrel and dancing." Miriam led the women in a praise dance in Exodus 15:20. Dancing was also a part of welcoming soldiers home from battle (Judg. 11:34). There was singing and dancing when David defeated Goliath (1 Sam. 18:6), and David danced before the Lord when they brought home the ark of the covenant (2 Sam. 6:14–15). The various art forms are well represented in Scripture.

Artists in the Bible

Maybe I'm biased, but I think God has a special place in his heart for artists, because so many are mentioned in the

Bible. Being an artist was one of the first occupations listed in the early days of the Old Testament, along with raising livestock and making tools (Gen. 4:20–22). There are several references to teams of musicians (Neh. 10:28–29; Ps. 150:3–5) and other artists (Ex. 31:2–6; 35:30–35). The worship team serving in the temple during David's reign was made up of 288 vocalists (1 Chron. 25:7). One of the judgments made against Babylon in the book of Revelation was that life would be void of the richness that artists bring (18:22).

Several artists are mentioned by name throughout Scripture. David, of course, was a skillful musician and songwriter (1 Sam. 16:18), described as a man after God's own heart. Solomon wrote more than one thousand songs (1 Kings 4:32). Kenaniah was a great vocalist and a song leader (1 Chron. 15:22). There is a group of musicians in 1 Chronicles whom I call the singing percussionists. Their names were Asaph, Heman, and Ethan (15:16–19), and they were vocalists who kept time for everyone by playing the cymbals. Bezalel was cited as a gifted visual artist (Ex. 35:30–33).

The Power of the Arts

I believe that the arts and artists are cited in Scripture because both play a vital role in the human experience. The arts can awaken us to truth and can change lives. In 1 Samuel 10, Saul encountered a group of musicians whose prophetic ministry was so powerful that Saul was "changed into a different person" (v. 6). That's the power of the arts! When the *Messiah* premiered in London, Lord Kinnoul congratulated Handel afterward on the excellent "entertainment." Like many of us, Handel bristled at the thought of his music being mere entertainment. "My Lord, I should be sorry if I only entertain them. I wish to make them better," he said.[9]

Scripture confirms that the arts can be especially powerful when anointed by the Holy Spirit. God used an anointed musician to open Elisha's heart to prophecy (2 Kings 3:15). An inspired piece of art in the hands of an anointed artist can be extremely powerful. An anointed song sung by a Spirit-filled vocalist results in a holy moment. We Christian artists can't do what we do apart from the one who gifted us. Let's never forget that our message is not in glitzy displays of our talent but in "a demonstration of the Spirit's power" (1 Cor. 2:4). One theme running through the book of Ezra is that God's hand was upon Ezra and all that he did. We need the mighty hand of the Lord to be upon all that we do. When God anoints the arts, he unleashes an awesome power to penetrate hearts, minds, and souls.

Artists in the Church

What kind of attitude should we artists have toward the church? Songwriter and producer Charlie Peacock believes that true artists "love the church despite indifference or opposition to their work. Though indifference is their enemy they separate it from the brother or sister who is seduced by it. They are eager to find their place in the body and do not consider themselves exempt from fellowship and church stewardship responsibilities. They love the church and do all they can to build it up, for how can you love Christ and hate his church?"[10] The church is called the bride of Christ because Jesus loves his church. And so should we!

Zac Hicks adds that "the local church is the hope of the world, because the church is the body of Christ, and Christ is the true hope of the world."[11] In spite of all its shortcomings (especially when it comes to the arts and artists), the church is still God's vehicle to redeem a lost world. If you want to invest your time and talent in something that pays eternal dividends, look no farther than your local church.

We live in a time, however, when many Christian artists don't give the church a second thought. When we think of using our art to impact the world, we usually don't think of doing that through the church. Or if we do, we see the church as a stepping-stone to something with a wider audience. A number of young people are growing up with the idea that real music ministry is found not in the church but in the Christian music industry. Yet the alto in the church choir, the Christian actor involved in community theater, and the born-again art professor are all every bit as much a Christian artist as someone in the industry. If you're doing church music but would rather be doing something else (like making it in the Christian music industry), don't do church music. Do something else. That goes for all of us artists. Don't look at the church as a stepping-stone to something you deem more important. Serve God at your church with passion and enthusiasm.

I don't want people to conclude that I think the church is the only acceptable avenue for a Christian to use his or her God-given talents. You need to find the right audience for your work, and it may not always be the church. Not every work of art fits into a church service. God calls some artists to use their gifts at their church, some out in the world, and some in both arenas. Follow God's leading in your life.

Why All the Fuss about Artists?

Some may be wondering why I'm focusing exclusively on the spiritual life of the artist. Aren't all Christians supposed to be growing spiritually and developing godly character? Yes, they are. But I believe artists merit special attention because of the unique needs of the artistic temperament and the high profile of artists in the church today.

UNIQUE NEEDS OF THE ARTIST

Author Barbara Nicolosi captures brilliantly the uniqueness of artistic people.

> I love artists and creative people. They make me crazy, but they're rarely boring. When they do get boring, it's because they are working on something they are so passionate about that they become obsessive. An artist caught up in an idea is like an eighteen-wheeler stuck in the sand, just grinding its wheels over and over. It can go on for months! But even when they are boring this way, it is fascinating because being passionate and obsessive is still an intense way of being alive and present to the beauty and complexity of life. When you're around artists, you are around people who are definitely living life to the fullest. Even their despair is gritty and real and fully committed.[12]

While Nicolosi accentuates the positive traits of artists, she also hints at some of the negative aspects. Living life to the fullest, for example, could lead to disaster if we're not careful. On the positive side, it means that we artists seek to experience all that life has to offer. The downside is that when you live in a fallen world, all that life has to offer is not always good for you. Some of it can ruin your life.

My artistic friend, you have outstanding abilities and amazing talents. Beware, though, because sometimes your greatest strengths can be your gravest weaknesses. If you're not careful, what makes you a great artist can work against you psychologically, emotionally, and spiritually. Certain aspects of the artistic temperament can make you successful as an artist but sabotage your marriage, your ministry, and your life. That's one reason why many artists, entertainers, and celebrities flame out and self-destruct. It's because they never learned how to manage the strengths and weaknesses—the ups and downs—of being an artist.

Some of us have strong feelings. We're in touch with our emotions, and that can be a wonderful trait. But if you let them control you, if you allow yourself to be ruled by your emotions, you will make bad decisions, misread people, and end up out of touch with reality. Some of us are sensitive by nature, and that too is a valuable strength. Many with artistic temperaments have been told to develop a thicker skin. That's nonsense! The world doesn't need more thick-skinned people. It needs more people like you who are sensitive and tender. So don't lose your sensitivity, especially to other people. But be careful that you don't become overly sensitive, easily offended, or chronically defensive. Last, as an artist, you have sophisticated taste. You have a stylishly nuanced analytical streak that enables you to make discriminating artistic choices. Maybe you've been told that you have a critical eye or a critical ear. Just make sure that you don't carry that critical, negative spirit into your relationships or your job and become overly critical of yourself and others. I believe that a holistic approach to spiritual formation in the life of the artist takes into account the uniqueness of the artistic temperament.

HIGH-PROFILE ARTISTS

Artists are some of the most visible people in the church today, especially for churches doing contemporary worship. Who is the first person that visitors see up front on the platform? Usually the worship leader. Where do visitors get their first impression of your church? From the worship team. Who gets stopped at the grocery store because someone recognized them from church? Worship ministry volunteers. Artists have a high profile in today's church. In many cases the worship leader has as much face time with the congregation as the pastor.

Serving God as an artist, whether it's out in the world or in the church, is a high and noble calling. God is reconciling a lost world to himself, and he invites you and me to be a part of this "ministry of reconciliation" (2 Cor. 5:18). What an honor! What a privilege! Let's be people God can trust with such a vital calling (1 Cor. 4:2). May the God who blessed you with artistic talent continue to grow you into the God-glorifying artist he created you to be.

CHAPTER 1

PROVEN CHARACTER

SEAN IS BOTH EXCITED AND NERVOUS. He recently finished Bible college, and now he's sitting in his first job interview. Sean's always dreamed of being a worship leader; he applied for positions at several churches across the country, hoping to find the perfect fit. Pastor Blair from Smalltown Community Church responded right away to Sean's application. They had several conversations over the phone and felt it was time to meet face-to-face. So here they are—Sean and Pastor Blair having lunch at the best restaurant in town. The meeting is going well. Sean is making a good impression.

"I think you're the best man for the job!" gushes the pastor. They both laugh. At that point Pastor Blair realizes he's been monopolizing the conversation. "I've been asking all the questions," he says, chuckling. "Do you have any questions for me, Sean?"

"Just a couple," replies Sean as he checks his phone. "I wrote them down so I wouldn't forget."

"Sure, go ahead," says Blair.

"I'm curious about the volunteers in the worship ministry. How are they doing? I understand they haven't had a leader for a while now. How's morale on the team?" That was a question Sean's college professor suggested he ask.

"I'll be honest with you," Pastor Blair responds, "morale has always been a major problem for us."

"What do you mean?"

"I hear there's a lot of bickering behind the scenes," Blair admits, shaking his head.

"You mean during sound check?"

"Yes, and at rehearsal and in the green room. You know how temperamental artists can be," he says with a slight smirk. "We've got some real characters on that team."

"Like who?" Sean is curious.

"Well, there's Theresa, who's been with us for who knows how long. She's pretty negative and contrary, doesn't take kindly to change, and will probably push back on any new ideas you try to introduce. She's been the face of our worship ministry for years, so she carries a lot of weight around the church. I suggest you get on her good side or you might have a rough go of it."

"Oh," says Sean, pensive.

"Then there's Travis, our guitar player. He can be rather feisty at times and downright defensive. You don't want to cross him; he's been known to curse up a blue streak when he's upset. He had it out with the last worship leader in front of the whole team once."

"Does that happen a lot?" Sean asks. "I don't know what I would do if a volunteer blew up at me."

"If he flies off the handle, don't take it personally," says Pastor Blair, rolling his eyes. "Just let him vent—that's what I do. It'll all blow over after a couple days."

Sean is quiet, so the pastor continues. "Then there's Miles, who is one of our newer vocalists, but I can't tell you much about him other than he's got a great voice. He used to sing professionally, I think, but he's rather undependable. We don't know from one week to the next whether he's going to show up. I don't know if he travels a lot or if he's just not committed to the church.

"Then there's Andy and Megan, a young couple who just moved here, but I sense they might be having marriage problems."

Sean is concerned. "Are they seeing a counselor or is anybody helping them?"

"Well, to be honest with you," says Pastor Blair, "I really don't think that's any of our business."

Sean is puzzled, but he remembers some practical matters

he wants to investigate. "Does the church have much in the way of sound equipment?"

"No," Pastor Blair says, smiling. "We're a pretty small church. We don't have the latest and greatest technical gadgets. We just get by with whatever the Lord gives us. We do have a sound system, of course. Nothing fancy, but it gets the job done."

Sean leans forward. "Does anybody know how to run it?"

"Oh yeah. His name is Wilbur. We call him Will for short. If I were you, I'd call him early every Sunday morning. He tends to oversleep."

"Is he a good sound man?" Sean presses, a little worried.

"Sure," Pastor Blair assures him. "I mean, there's really nothing to it, right? You just flip on a few switches and we're good to go."

Sean laughs nervously. He's concerned about asking too many questions, but he's also curious about whether there are any other artists in the church. "Do you have anyone at the church who draws or paints?"

Pastor Blair pauses to think. "I can't think of anybody," he says. "We do have a craft fair before Christmas every year."

Sean is a little dazed. He went into this interview with high hopes and great expectations, but now he has mixed emotions. "It seems like whoever gets the job at your church is going to have their hands full," he says quietly.

"You're right about that, son!" says Pastor Blair. "It's not a job for the weak of heart, but I think you'll do just fine."

Questions for Group Discussion

1. If you were Sean, would you take the job at Smalltown Community Church? Why or why not?
2. What do you think Sean's first year would be like if he accepted this job?
3. Do you think Sean and Pastor Blair would make a good team? Why or why not?
4. The worship ministry at Pastor Blair's church seems to have some "problem people." How would you handle them?
5. Do you think the problems in the worship department at Pastor Blair's church are extreme or typical of many churches?
6. Does the church have any obligation to those who are going through difficult times, like the couple who is having marriage problems?
7. What would it take for the arts to thrive in a church like Pastor Blair's?
8. What would it take for artists to thrive in this church?

Character

People sometimes ask me what I would do if I had to choose between a highly talented musician who isn't very spiritual and a deeply spiritual one who isn't very talented. I think that question captures the dilemma the church has been in with artists for a long time. My answer is, I want both! I want artists who are highly talented and deeply spiritual.

There was an artist in Exodus 35 named Bezalel who was gifted in sculpting things out of gold, silver, bronze, stone, and wood. He was a visual artist who was innovative and creative. He was also filled with the Holy Spirit in wisdom, understanding, and knowledge (vv. 30–31). This spiritual giant also had teaching gifts. He was an artist who was both talented and godly. That's what we need to be shooting for! That's the biblical standard. We can't expect to get by on talent alone. It's imperative that we keep growing spiritually and artistically.

The Greek philosopher Heraclitus taught that a person's character is their destiny. That's a value shift for artists because we tend to think that our destiny is all wrapped up in our talent. But our destiny doesn't hinge entirely on what we do as artists; it hinges on who we are as people. John Wooden, the legendary college basketball coach, warns us to "be more concerned with your character than with your reputation, because your character is what you really are while your reputation is merely what others think you are."[13] So who are you really? Who are you when you're not up on the platform? Who are you when you're not in the spotlight? Who are you when no one's looking?

Romans 5 says that our perseverance results in proven character (vv. 3–4). God wants to develop us into artists of proven character. Building character simply means that we're trying to become the people God wants us to be—in our case, the artists God wants us to be. N. T. Wright defines character as the pattern of thinking and acting that we consistently display; the opposite is superficiality, where someone appears, at first glance, to be virtuous, but when you get to know them better, you realize they're not nearly as virtuous as they seem.[14] Godly character is consistent; it's proven to be the general direction of our lives. It does not vacillate between acting virtuously one minute and acting egregiously the next. I'm not talking about being perfect. I'm referring to a depth of character that's proven over time to be true to the life God has called us to live.

What does proven character look like? Paul says that our lives should demonstrate "love, which comes from a pure heart and a good conscience and a sincere faith" (1 Tim. 1:5). A person with character is loving, has a clear conscience, and has an authentic relationship with the Lord. These are telltale signs of someone with godly character.

Are we becoming more loving people, or are we too

wrapped up in ourselves or our art? Are we loving the Lord with all our heart, soul, and mind? Or is it singing, playing, acting, or creating that is truly our first love? Would those around you say that you're a loving person?

Do we have a clear conscience about how we're living our lives? Are we honest people? Are we dealing with sin in our lives, or are we hiding it? Are we living as those who are dead to sin and alive to Christ, or are we giving in to the passing pleasures of sin? Are we accountable to someone concerning our sin?

Are we living authentic lives as followers of Christ? The Bible refers to authenticity as living a life of truth in our "innermost being" (Ps. 51:6 NASB) and living a life of "godly sincerity" (2 Cor. 1:12). That means we are who we say we are. We're living what we sing about. We're living what we write about. People won't listen to what we say until they have watched what we do and found consistency. Some of us try to hide behind our talents, and we neglect who we are on the inside, but who we are deep inside is who we really are. That's why Paul says that he tries to keep a clear conscience before God and in his dealings with other people (Acts 24:16).

Like Paul, we don't want to be accused of not practicing what we preach. That's hypocrisy—when we look good on the outside for the sake of looking good onstage but it's not really who we are on the inside. We know the right words to say to come off "Christianly," but we're covering up the truth about ourselves. It's merely a "form of godliness" (2 Tim. 3:5). It looks spiritual but has no depth or power. It happens when we sing about giving our all for Jesus but live to satisfy ourselves. In Amos 5:23, God calls his people to task because what they are singing doesn't match how they are living: "Away with the noise of your songs! I will not listen to the music of your harps." God won't listen to empty songs of praise, no matter how creative or beautiful they are. Our hearts must be right as we worship him. The Bible describes King Amaziah as a man who "did what was right in the eyes of the Lord, but not wholeheartedly" (2 Chron. 25:2). Amaziah's actions were good, but his attitude was bad. He looked good on the outside, but his heart was far from God. Is your heart on fire for Christ these days, or are you just going through the motions?

Authenticity is a powerful witness to the presence of God in our lives. It doesn't mean that we're perfect. It means that we're real, that we're honest about our struggles and shortcomings. We don't gloss over our flaws and put on a happy Christian face. Authenticity means that we admit our struggles and shortcomings and deal with them.

God never intended our character growth to be a low priority. We are all supposed to mature spiritually "to the whole measure of the fullness of Christ" (Eph. 4:13). We are to grow up "in every respect" into Christ (v. 15). Growing in

Christ doesn't mean that we merely acquire head knowledge. It means that we grow in areas such as moral excellence, intimacy with Christ, self-control and discipline, perseverance, godliness, kindness, and love (2 Peter 1:5–7). "If you possess these qualities in increasing measure, they will keep you from being ineffective and unproductive in your knowledge of our Lord Jesus Christ" (v. 8). This is the stuff from which character is built.

Any time and energy given to growing in godly character is well worth the effort. Character growth will improve our relationship with God. It'll improve our relationships with friends and family. It'll improve our relationships with the people we work with. It'll improve our overall well-being. We will be better artists for having grown in character.

Integrity

Character is becoming who God made us to be. Integrity is doing what God wants us to do. In Psalm 101:2, David says, "I will walk within my house in the integrity of my heart" (NASB). We artists need to be able to walk through the church lobby with integrity in our hearts. Integrity simply means doing what's right in God's eyes. Even if it's difficult, even if it jeopardizes our careers, even if no one else is doing it. People of integrity want to conduct themselves honorably in all things (Heb. 13:18). They try to be good examples in all things (Titus 2:7) and please God above all else (2 Cor. 8:21). We need to conduct all our affairs with integrity, to treat all people with love and respect, to speak truth and be devoted to honesty. We need to manage our ministries, our careers, our finances, and our homes with integrity. Our thoughts, our words, our deeds must reflect a desire to do what's right in the eyes of God.

Paul says that his greatest ambition is to please God (2 Cor. 5:9). Is that your greatest ambition? Are you living to please God, or are you living to please yourself? Are you trying to bring a smile to God's face with your talents, or is your main goal to gratify yourself artistically? When it comes to integrity, there is a high road and there is a low road. We need to make sure we're always taking the high road. We don't need the congregation viewing us as a bunch of narcissistic artists; they need to see us as people of integrity who minister, serve, and shepherd in the powerful name of Jesus. First Timothy 4:12 says that we are to be model examples "in speech, in conduct, in love, in faith and in purity."

Some of us have grown up with high standards attached to the pastor and the elders but not to the artists leading worship. We expect pastors to be godly people. We expect them to walk intimately with Christ and have godly character. We expect them to be living in righteousness and not leading a double life. Why don't we expect the same from our musicians and all our other artists? We're not just artists.

We are ministers too. We stand on the same platform and address the congregation with the same message. Shouldn't we aspire to high standards of integrity just like the pastor?

The qualifications for elders in 1 Timothy 3 and Titus 1 can be applied to all leaders in the church, including the artists who lead worship every week. We are to be above reproach, loyal to our spouses, temperate, prudent, respectable, hospitable, able to teach, not self-willed or quick-tempered, not addicted to anything, not pugnacious but gentle, uncontentious, free from the love of money, and able to manage our households well, and we must have a good reputation with those outside the church (1 Tim. 3:2–7; Titus 1:7–9).

The early church required everyone who served to exemplify a life of integrity. All who ministered were to be reputed for being "full of the Spirit and wisdom" (Acts 6:3), people of integrity and high character. This wasn't the standard for high-profile positions only; it was the standard for all servants in the church. Likewise, those of us who serve in the worship ministry need to be people of integrity and proven character. Lewis Smedes insists that integrity "is about being a certain kind of person. It is about being people who know who we are and what we are, and it is about being true to what we are even when it could cost us more than we should like to pay."[15] An artist of godly integrity lives in a way that is congruent with what he or she claims to believe.

Psalm 4:3 notes that the Lord sets apart godly people for

himself. Godly artists have been set apart with a special gift or a unique talent, set apart to experience intimacy with the Lord, set apart to be used by God to accomplish his mission in the world. I believe that God wants to raise up artists in the church who are set apart for him. They're not different in a strange way, like so many artists in the world. They're different because they're artists with godly character who live lives of integrity. They're not only talented; they're humble, loving, and approachable. They walk with God. They're so sold out to Jesus that people don't stand in awe of their talent; they stand in awe of their God (Luke 9:43).

Testing Brings Growth

How does one go about growing in character? We grow when our character gets tested (1 Peter 1:7). As Paul describes, "Tribulation brings about perseverance; and perseverance, proven character" (Rom. 5:3–4 NASB). Tribulation, or testing, produces perseverance, and perseverance molds our character. When we encounter difficulty, it demands a response. We can be pulled along by the darker side of our human nature, or we can respond with integrity. The way we respond to certain challenges and even certain thoughts that pop into our minds goes a long way in shaping our character. Growing in character starts with a decision to respond with integrity when facing the challenges of life.

One day a pastor asked me to join his worship staff for lunch. They were planting a new church and wanted to pick my brain about worship. These two music guys were bright, energetic, and committed. We had a lively discussion, and I was impressed by the depth of their questions and comments. As our lunch appointment drew to a close, the pastor asked me if I had any parting words of wisdom for "these two young bucks." As gently as I could, I warned them that being in ministry would test their character as it had never been tested before. I encouraged them to "press on to maturity" (Heb. 6:1 NASB), to let God have his way and mold them into the godly artists he wanted them to be.

Ministry will test and perfect godly character and integrity in all artists. Our character gets tested when we're asked to play a behind-the-scenes role instead of the more prominent role we wanted to play. Our character gets tested when someone gives us constructive criticism. Our character gets tested every time our feelings get hurt. Our character gets tested when perfectionism rears its ugly head and we're tempted to come down hard on ourselves and others for not living up to our expectations. Our character gets tested when a situation calls for us to put the needs of others ahead of our own. Our character gets tested when we face the temptation to sin, when we try to meet our needs apart from God. How we respond to these little tests determines whether we will become artists of godly character and integrity.

Taking Inventory

How are you doing these days in terms of your character growth? Where are you strong and what areas need attention? One of the crucial steps in any recovery program is to take a moral inventory of yourself. Paul recommends this in 2 Corinthians 13:5 when he instructs us to examine and test ourselves to see whether we are truly in the faith (see also 1 Cor. 11:28). His most passionate plea on the subject comes from 1 Timothy 4:14–16: "Do not neglect your gift, which was given you through prophecy when the body of elders laid their hands on you. Be diligent in these matters; give yourself wholly to them, so that everyone may see your progress. Watch your life and doctrine closely. Persevere in them." Paul is using very strong language to exhort us to grow and become the people God wants us to be. Perhaps Paul was so adamant because of our tendency to avoid honest self-reflection. We'd rather judge others than evaluate ourselves.

To avoid being too hard or too easy on ourselves, we must include God in the process. We should pray as David does in Psalm 139:23–24: "Search me, God, and know my heart; test me and know my anxious thoughts. See if there is any offensive way in me, and lead me in the way everlasting." Take inventory on where your character growth is these days. We'll be addressing each of these areas in the remainder of this book, but for now answer the following questions as honestly as you can.

SERVANTHOOD

1. How often do you put the needs of others ahead of your own?
    a. Most often.
    b. Sometimes.
    c. I hardly ever think about it.

2. How did you respond the last time you were asked to serve out of the spotlight and behind the scenes?
    a. I did it with joy.
    b. I didn't like it, but I did it anyway.
    c. It made me angry.

TEAMWORK

1. Are you using your artistic talents at church and experiencing genuine community with a group of Christian artists?
    a. Yes.
    b. I'm not currently serving at church.
    c. I have no meaningful relationships with other Christian artists.

2. How are you at resolving relational conflict in your life?
    a. I always try to go straight to the individual and talk.
    b. Most of the time I try to talk it out with the person.
    c. I hate confrontation, so I suppress my feelings when people hurt me.

PERFECTIONISM

1. Do you entertain thoughts in your head that you're not good enough as an artist?
    a. Not very often.
    b. Sometimes.
    c. Just about all the time.

2. Are you hard on yourself when you make a mistake?
    a. No.
    b. Sometimes.
    c. Yes, I can be very hard on myself.

DEFENSIVENESS

1. Has anyone ever said that they feel as if they have to walk on eggshells around you?
    a. Never.
    b. Sometimes.
    c. I hear that from people all the time.

2. How do you respond to constructive criticism?
    a. I welcome feedback and regularly invite it from others.
    b. It's hard, but I usually accept it with grace.
    c. I feel hurt.

JEALOUSY AND ENVY

1. How do you respond to someone with more talent or success than you?
    a. I praise God for bestowing talent on that person and for gifting me as well.
    b. It's hard, but I try not to let it affect me.
    c. I turn inward and feel inadequate and inferior.

2. When you run across someone with more talent or success than you, does it make you want to give up being an artist?
    a. Never.
    b. Sometimes.
    c. Often.

MANAGING YOUR EMOTIONS

1. Has anyone ever told you that you're too negative or moody?
    a. Never.
    b. Sometimes.
    c. I hear that often.

2. Do you ever sense that you're being controlled by your emotions?
    a. Never.
    b. Sometimes.
    c. Yes, I often feel controlled by my emotions.

LEADING ARTISTS

1. If you're a leader who is also an artist, do you ever sense any tension between the two roles?
   a. No, never.
   b. Sometimes.
   c. Yes, I don't see how I can adequately fulfill both roles.

2. If you lead a team of artists, how well are they following you?
   a. I feel inept at leading artists.
   b. We've got conflict on the team and I don't know how to resolve it.
   c. We all seem to be moving together in the right direction.

SIN

1. Are there any ongoing sins or bad habits in your life right now?
   a. No.
   b. No, but there are a couple of areas in which I struggle at times.
   c. I'm struggling with a certain sin, and I don't know what to do about it.

2. Do you have anybody in your life to whom you're accountable regarding sin?
    a. Yes.
    b. I have accountability in my life, but it's not strong or consistent.
    c. I have no accountable relationships in my life right now.

SPIRITUAL DISCIPLINES

1. Do you have a regular quiet time with the Lord or practice regular devotions?
    a. Yes.
    b. I try, but it's hard for me to be consistent.
    c. I'm just not very disciplined in this area.

2. Do you feel that you have a good relationship with the Lord these days?
    a. My relationship with God is going well.
    b. I'm feeling dry spiritually these days.
    c. I feel far away from the Lord right now.

Committing to a Process

God works in our lives to conform us to the image of Christ (Rom. 8:29). Dante says that we are worms destined to be angelic butterflies. This metamorphosis doesn't happen overnight; it takes time. I wish I could say that character growth is quick and easy. But when it comes to the transformation of your character, you're most often going against the grain of who you are naturally and how you were brought up, so it's no easy task. We don't like anything that hurts or takes time. We roll our eyes whenever we encounter anything difficult, saying, "Well, I guess it'll build character," as if it's medicine that's good for us but tastes bad. In spite of the challenges and difficulties, I invite you to embrace the process. Do everything you can to cooperate with the Lord's efforts to mold you and shape your character.

As we learned in Romans 5:3–4, the tribulation that leads to perseverance results in proven character. Character growth is a sweet gift. It's God's reward for our being faithful and persevering through the arduous journey of spiritual formation. There will be highs and there will be lows. Most of the time it'll be two steps forward and one backward. Paul never felt that he had arrived. He said, "Forgetting what is behind and straining toward what is ahead, I press on toward the goal to win the prize for which God has called me heavenward in Christ Jesus" (Phil. 3:13–14). In spite of his failures and disappointments, Paul stayed committed to the process of growing in character.

My artistic friend, I invite you on a lifelong, life-changing journey. It's going to call for day-to-day commitment to die to self and follow God (Luke 9:23; John 12:24). It might be humbling as God brings to light things in your character that need to be changed. It might be painful as God surgically removes whatever is holding you back from being all he wants you to be. But there will be wonderful breakthroughs along the way. Our God is a God of breakthroughs (2 Sam. 5:20). He's working in us "to will and to act in order to fulfill his good purpose" (Phil. 2:13). He began a good work in us and will bring it to completion (Phil. 1:6). He is able to make us what he wants us to be. So be patient with your progress and trust God with the outcome. You can begin by presenting yourself to God as an artist who is set apart for him. Commit today to become an artist of deep character and high integrity for God's glory.

Follow-Up Questions for Group Discussion

1. Does the phrase artistic temperament have a negative connotation for you? Why or why not?
2. What kind of art moves you the most?
3. In your opinion, what should the role of the arts be in church?
4. How can the church become more of a safe place for artists?
5. What's the best way for the church to help artists grow in character?
6. Share an area of your life that has changed since you became a Christian. How did that change happen?

7. Why is it hard for people to change?

8. What has helped you in the past to grow spiritually?

PERSONAL ACTION STEPS

1. Craft a prayer that expresses your desire to be set apart for God, to grow in Christlike character, and to be the person God created you to be.

2. In a concrete, public way, articulate or affirm your commitment to become an artist of godly character.

3. Choose for yourself a personal ministry verse—a Bible verse that reflects your passion and/or giftedness.

4. Considering the time and attention given to your artistic growth and your spiritual growth, determine which has been the bigger priority for you and prayerfully consider whether you need to rearrange your priorities.

5. Ask God to reveal to you any areas of your life (family relationships, finances, thoughts, attitudes, work ethic) that don't reflect godly character.

6. Go through the list of questions in the "Taking Inventory" section of this chapter and circle the question or topic that reveals the area of your character in which you want to see the most growth during the next year. Decide to whom you could be accountable to grow in that area.

CHAPTER 2

SERVANTHOOD VERSUS STARDOM

AMBER JOINED THE WORSHIP TEAM AT Main Street Community Church amid much fanfare. She had served at a megachurch in the city and recorded her own worship CD, so the pastor and the congregation felt fortunate to have such a gifted and accomplished musician leading their worship ministry. A year later, leaders at Main Street regretted putting Amber in leadership.

Amber's tenure at the church began with a bang. She and her megachurch friends led a worship concert at Main Street that was very well received. The church was packed that night and attendance the following Sunday skyrocketed. People commented on how much they loved Amber's voice and the strong stage presence she brought to worship.

But as time went on, Amber's star began to tarnish. Those who worked closely with her, especially the volunteers, perceived her as arrogant, and though no one would say it out loud, some even thought she was a prima donna. Amber was distant, hardly ever talking to or socializing with the other singers. She was often late for rehearsal, sometimes keeping people waiting for up to an hour. Sometimes she didn't make it to rehearsal and didn't even bother to call. When Amber did show up, she was rarely prepared, so rehearsals were disorganized and poorly run. Amber's antics during a sound check didn't exactly endear her to everyone either. She was impatient when the musicians struggled to learn their parts and was openly critical of the audio team. She often lost her temper and more than once stomped off the platform in a rage. Congregation members also noticed that Amber didn't sit through the pastor's messages and rarely attended any function of the church that didn't call for her to sing. Though everyone agreed that Amber had a great voice, they realized that she wasn't as nice and pleasant behind the scenes as she was when she was up front singing.

The pastor invited Amber several times to accompany him during his weekly hospital visits, but she always declined, explaining that she didn't do that sort of thing and that her real calling was to sing about Jesus to large groups of people. The pastor perceived a prima donna attitude in Amber and tried to take her aside and gently teach her about servanthood in ministry, but she became offended. She couldn't understand why the pastor was singling her out. "Doesn't the

Bible tell us not to judge?" she asked angrily. She was hurt. She felt misunderstood. *These people don't appreciate me*, she thought, so she left the church and never came back.

The church, by the way, recovered nicely and went on to have a dynamic worship ministry even without Amber.

Questions for Group Discussion

1. Amber would never call herself a prima donna, yet she was perceived as one. What behavior on her part communicated a greater-than-thou attitude?
2. Do you think the pastor did the right thing in confronting Amber about her attitude? Why or why not?
3. Should people like Amber be confronted, or should we leave them alone and tolerate them?
4. What makes it difficult to confront people like Amber?
5. How would you feel if you were one of the vocalists Amber reprimanded in front of everyone else? Or one of the instrumentalists she cut down? Or the sound technician she mistreated?
6. What is it about the stage and public ministry that makes it difficult for an artist to have a servant's heart?
7. In your opinion, what characterizes a true servant of Christ?

Servants or Stars?

I shared this scenario with someone outside the worship ministry, and her response was, "Isn't this extreme? Surely there aren't really people like Amber out there, right?" Those of us with experience in worship would likely admit that we've known an Amber or two sometime in our lives. But when we are honest with ourselves, we have to admit that there is a little bit of Amber in all of us. The desire to be served comes easier to us than the desire to serve. We artists can be very selfish and self-absorbed at times. We like the attention that our talents bring us. We like the feeling of specialness that comes with being gifted. Our society tends to put anybody who has talent on a pedestal. We turn the most successful artists into superstars. The superstars are indulged and pampered. They become rich and famous. So servanthood and being others-oriented doesn't come naturally for any of us.

Let's face it, servanthood is a countercultural notion; it goes against human nature. If given a choice, we'd all choose notoriety over obscurity. We'd rather be noticed and recognized than relegated to serve behind the scenes. I heard that someone once asked Leonard Bernstein what the most difficult instrument in the orchestra is to play. The great maestro thought for a second and replied, "Second fiddle." No one wants to play second fiddle; we'd all rather have the spotlight.

Three Barriers to True Servanthood

God's Word has a different standard for those of us who minister in his name. According to 1 Corinthians 4:1, people should recognize us as "servants of Christ." Do the people at our churches see us as servants or stars? Do they see us as ministers or entertainers? I contend that there are three barriers to true servanthood.

I. AN ATTITUDE OF SUPERIORITY

The first barrier is an attitude of superiority. Few Christians would say out loud that they're better than someone else, but we can communicate an attitude of superiority by the way we treat others. In our opening scenario, Amber never came out and said she was greater than everyone else. She didn't have to, because her actions gave her away. She was distant, she kept to herself, she didn't try to reach out to others, she was always late, she missed rehearsals without calling, she was impatient with the sound technician and other singers, she was sarcastic toward the band, she came to rehearsal unprepared, she didn't sit through the sermon, she didn't come to church unless she was singing, and she had an unteachable spirit. Amber clearly thought that courtesies and requirements demanded of everyone else were beneath her. Actions really do speak louder than words, don't they?

Behind this attitude of superiority is misguided pride. Pride is a hidden desire to be exalted. It's a serious sin that we need to be vigilant about. Pride unfortunately is also one of those sins that is so easy to see in others but not in ourselves. Off the top of our heads, each of us could probably name five people who we think have a pride problem. But the real question is, where is the sin of pride in your heart? How does pride manifest itself in your life?

Pride fosters a boastful, arrogant spirit. The Bible says that if you want to boast about someone (whether to yourself or out loud), boast about God (2 Cor. 10:17). Boast about God's sufficiency in your weakness (2 Cor. 12:9). Boasting is a coping mechanism to handle insecurity, but it tends to perpetuate the problem by preventing us from dealing with our deep-seated feelings of inferiority.

2. SELFISH ULTERIOR MOTIVES

The second barrier to true servanthood is selfish ulterior motives. We need to look deep and keep a watchful eye on our motives, because the Bible says the human heart is deceitful and "beyond cure" (Jer. 17:9). Each of us is fully capable of selfish motives. In Acts 8:17–24, we find a story about a man named Simon who had ulterior motives. Simon saw Peter and John laying hands on people and witnessing glorious manifestations of the Holy Spirit, and he wanted that power for selfish gain. He offered Peter and John money for this Holy Spirit power, but Peter rebuked him and commanded him to repent of his greedy ambitions.

We too need to repent of selfish ulterior motives. If we don't, we could think we're serving God and actually be serving ourselves. Sometimes our interior motive is to get attention or to be noticed. We crave approval, validation, or applause. Or we want to be recognized. When our agenda is "me, me, me," we have selfish motives. It happens whenever we manipulate the topic of conversation to come around to us and our talent. It happens when we name-drop to make ourselves look important. It happens when we talk about our accomplishments to prove our worth. What's driving us in those moments is selfish ulterior motives.

3. SELF-SUFFICIENCY

The third barrier to true servanthood occurs when we put all our confidence in our giftedness, our natural talent. In Philippians 3:3, Paul insists that his confidence is in Christ, not in himself. People who are gifted and talented always run the risk of thinking and acting like they don't need the Lord. They're so good at what they do that they can become self-sufficient if they're not careful.

If we think we can make it on our own because we're smart enough or talented enough, we're sadly mistaken. Sometimes a vocalist feels a cold coming on just before he or she is to record or perform in concert. At times like this, our confidence is not in our talent but in the power of God to use us in our weakness. When artists have more confidence in their giftedness than in the Lord, they leave the platform more worried about how they looked or sounded than about whether God used them. They're more concerned with technique than with substance. They're focused on their own glory rather than on God's glory.

Christ's Example of Servanthood

Jesus of course is the ultimate example of servanthood. Mark 10:45 says that "even the Son of Man did not come to be served, but to serve, and to give his life as a ransom for many." In Philippians 2, Paul describes how Jesus "made himself nothing by taking the very nature of a servant" (v. 7) and "humbled himself by becoming obedient" (v. 8). The Son of God left the glory and privilege of heaven to be born in a remote, backward little country at a technologically primitive point in time. After two thousand years, the picture of Jesus washing the disciples' feet is etched in our minds, yet we still fail to understand all that it means.

Jesus was a radical departure from the cold, distant, self-centered gods of the ancient Greeks and Romans. His model of servanthood goes against the grain of human history, in which leaders have always ruled through domination. To lead by serving goes against human nature. Can you imagine what it would be like to have Jesus in your worship ministry? What would it be like to have Jesus on your tech team or in the choir or on the visual arts team?

Jesus would be a servant artist. He said it himself: "The greatest among you will be your servant" (Matt. 23:11). If you need a visual aid to inspire you to serve others, picture Jesus washing the feet of the disciples (John 13:2–15). There's an awkward beauty to that scene, isn't there? In a world where might is right, Jesus, the Son of God, was willing to wash dirty feet. Imagine the God of the universe washing your feet. That's true servanthood!

Have you ever washed someone's feet? It's a humbling experience. When my two sons were younger, every year I would wash their feet during Holy Week to remind myself to be a loving servant father and to remind them to serve each other. Every year, I was struck with just how humbling and awkward menial tasks of service can be. Jesus humbled himself and embraced the awkwardness of servanthood.

Embracing Humility

Servanthood starts with humility. Humility means moving from self-centeredness to God-centeredness. Before we talk about what humility is, let's delve into what it's not. True humility is not cutting yourself down or letting people walk all over you. That's false humility. Romans 12:3 cautions us not to think more highly of ourselves than we ought but to regard ourselves with "sober judgment." Don't think of yourself more highly than you should, and don't think of yourself more lowly than you should. Sometimes a bad self-image is mistaken for humility. True humility is not thinking so poorly of yourself that you lack confidence, boldness, or assertiveness. You may think it's fashionable or even spiritual to cut yourself down or to minimize your gifts or to keep quiet because you don't think your ideas are worth sharing, but that's counterfeit humility. And it's wrong because it denies that you matter to God. It contradicts Scripture and violates God's character. Don't beat yourself down and call it humility.

In C. S. Lewis's classic book *The Screwtape Letters*, two demons, Screwtape and Wormwood, discuss a strategy to ensnare human beings in this false type of humility. This is Screwtape talking to his fellow demon:

> You must therefore conceal from the patient the true end of humility. Let him think of it, not as self-forgetfulness, but as a certain kind of opinion (namely, a low opinion) of his own talents and character. Some talents, I gather, he really has. Fix in his mind the idea that humility consists in trying to believe those talents to be less valuable than he believes them to be. . . . The great thing is to make him value an opinion for some quality other than truth, thus

> introducing an element of dishonesty and make-believe into the heart of what otherwise threatens to become a virtue. By this method thousands of humans have been brought to think that humility means pretty women trying to believe they are ugly and clever men trying to believe they are fools. And since what they are trying to believe may, in some cases, be manifest nonsense, they cannot succeed in believing it, and we have the chance of keeping their minds endlessly revolving on themselves in an effort to achieve the impossible.[16]

Regarding ourselves with sound judgment helps avoid false humility.

True humility means having an accurate view of ourselves, thinking we're no more or less than we are. Know your strengths and accept your weaknesses. Acknowledge what you're good at and recognize where you need to improve.

Let's discuss how to embrace true humility as an artist.

HUMBLE YOURSELF BEFORE GOD

First, humble yourself before God. Jesus said that "all those who exalt themselves will be humbled, and those who humble themselves will be exalted" (Luke 18:14). James 4:10 also commends humility. Scripture contends that God has a special place in his heart for the humble, that he dwells with the "contrite and lowly in spirit" (Isa. 57:15), and that he "looks kindly on the lowly" (Ps. 138:6; see also Isa. 66:2).

Pride, on the other hand, is an abomination to the Lord (Prov. 16:5). The Bible says that God is opposed to the proud (1 Peter 5:5). He resists those who think they're better than everyone else (James 4:6). Think about how serious an offense pride is to the Lord. You don't want God opposed to you and your ministry, do you? Psalm 138:6 says, "The haughty He knows from afar" (NASB). God tends to distance himself from the proud, to stand far away and aloof. What a dreadful thought! Pride, self-centeredness, and a lack of humility are not pleasing to God. It's imperative that we humble ourselves before God, because apart from him we can do nothing (John 15:4–5).

Remember that your talent comes from God. You're developing it, but he gave it to you. Before they entered the promised land, Moses warned the people of Israel not to forget that all their blessings were a gift from God. This is what Moses might say to us artists today: "Be humble about your talent. Otherwise you may say in your heart that you did it all on your own. But you shall remember the Lord your God, for it is he who gave you the ability to do what you do" (Deut. 8:17–18, my paraphrase).

If you and I accomplish anything artistically, it's because of a gift or talent that came from God. "By the grace of God I am what I am," admits Paul (1 Cor. 15:10). We of all people have every reason to be humble before God and others. That's why Philippians 3:3 warns us not to put our confidence in the flesh, because our confidence is in God. Humility comes naturally to the person who places all of his or her confidence in God. The writer of Ecclesiastes labels as a fool someone who boasts, "My heart took delight in all *my* labor, and this was the reward for all *my* toil" (2:10, my emphasis). The prideful person announces, "Look what I did." The humble person says, "Look at what God did through me."

HUMBLE YOURSELF BEFORE OTHERS

First Peter 5:5 tells us to clothe ourselves with humility toward one another. We are to abandon any thoughts of superiority that would cause us to think we deserve special treatment. Arrogance has no place in the heart of a Christian artist.

David was as much a celebrity in Israel as one could be. He had success, fame, and fortune, but he didn't let it go to his head. The Bible says that "all Israel and Judah loved David, and he went out and came in before them" (1 Sam. 18:16 NASB). The Living Bible says that "he was as one of them." Even though he was rich and famous, he was approachable; he was still just one of the guys. David was humble before others.

Sometimes, in the process of using our talents, we artists

get elevated higher than we should. Praise for the artist can be effusive for many reasons—the glory of the spotlight, the impact of the arts, the rarity of the gifts. People say things like, "I love your voice more than anyone else's I've ever heard" or "I don't know how you do it; you're amazing." How do you respond to that kind of adulation?

I've heard people (myself included) string together a bunch of Christian clichés in an effort to sound spiritual. The result sounds something like, "Oh, it wasn't really me out there. I had nothing to do with it. It was all God. Praise the Lord. I just open my mouth, and he takes over." Such a response sounds flippant. Then there are those who don't know how to respond to praise without cutting themselves down. They figure false humility is better than no humility at all. Their response goes something like this: "I'm just a sinful worm filling in until God finds somebody better to do the job."

Oftentimes the best response is a simple and humble, "Thank you." The Bible says that the way we respond to praise reflects our character (Prov. 27:21). Do we let the praise that's heaped on us cause us to think we're better than other people? Do we really give God the glory, or do we just say the appropriate Christian things so it appears we're giving God the glory? Jesus reminds us in Luke 17:10 that when we use our gifts for him, "we have only done our duty." In God's economy there is no hierarchy of gifts and talents (1 Cor. 12:22–23). Just because we're up front or performing onstage, that doesn't mean we're any better than anyone else who's faithfully using his or her gifts in the church.

This is not to say that it's wrong to feel good about ourselves or about something we've done. It is quite all right to take pleasure in pleasing God with our talents. That should be one of our main ambitions in life (2 Cor. 5:9). But some of us get very uncomfortable when someone applauds our efforts or pays us a compliment. We haven't learned how to receive a compliment with grace. We don't know how to handle it because we don't think it's okay for people to thank us or say nice things about what we do. Luke 17:10 shows us that Jesus is assuming that people will commend us if we do well, so don't try to squelch it. Receive it with humility. Remember that when we use our gifts and talents for the Lord, we're only doing what we ought to be doing. So graciously acknowledge and thank those who encourage you.

The great composer Franz Joseph Haydn was reputed to be a humble man. One time an admirer was fawning over him, and he responded by saying, "Do not speak so to me. You see only a man whom God has granted talent and a good heart."[17] Haydn responded with gracious humility that pointed people to God.

DIE TO YOUR DESIRE TO BE THE GREATEST

In addition to humbling ourselves before God and others, we need to die to the desire to be the greatest. How do we know whether we have a servant's heart? There's a saying that we can tell how much of a servant we are by how we respond to being treated like one. Unfortunately, most of us get all bent out of shape if we're not treated as if we're special. C. S. Lewis says, "Pride gets no pleasure out of having something, only out of having more of it than the next man. We say that people are proud of being rich, or clever, or good looking, but they are not. They are proud of being richer, or cleverer, or better looking than others. If everyone else became equally rich, or clever, or good looking there would be nothing to be proud about. It is the comparison that makes you proud: the pleasure of being above the rest."[18]

For many of us, it's not enough to be talented. We want to be the most talented. There was a man named Diotrephes who brought disgrace to himself and the church because he was so intent on being prominent that he loved "to be first" (3 John 9). The disciples struggled with this too, arguing about who among them was the greatest (Luke 9:46–48; 22:24–30).

We may laugh at them now, but the same selfish desire lurks deep inside many of us. Instead of being the best we can be, we want to be top dog in our group or church. But ministry is not a popularity contest, and jockeying for position is wrong for Christ's followers. Jesus is the head of the church, and he is to have first place in everything (Col. 1:18). When you and I die to our need to be noticed, we'll fulfill an even greater need: the need for significance in God's eyes. Exchange self-importance for a life of true significance.

The Servant Artist

Worship artists today can get a distorted view of servanthood because, aside from the tech team, we serve in the spotlight rather than behind the scenes. We could even be deceived into thinking our service is altruistic, when in reality it's ego driven. How can we avoid such self-deception? I suggest we follow the example set by the artists who served under Nehemiah.

The Old Testament reveals that in Nehemiah's day the musicians were in charge of maintenance for the house of God (Neh. 11:22–23). These janitors-by-day/artists-by-night had a strict, disciplined daily routine that included doing the custodial work needed for the upkeep of God's house. These servant artists demonstrated humility by serving others. According to Richard Foster, "Nothing disciplines the inordinate desires of the flesh like service, and nothing transforms the desires of the flesh like serving in hiddenness. The flesh whines against service but screams against hidden service. It strains and pulls for honor and recognition. It will devise subtle, religiously acceptable means to call attention to the service rendered. If we stoutly refuse to give in to this lust of the flesh, we crucify it. Every time we crucify the flesh, we crucify our pride and arrogance."[19] Serving others transforms our character.

How can those of us in worship ministry today emulate the servant artists of Nehemiah's day? I have five suggestions.

1. FOCUS ON PEOPLE

First, stay focused on ministering to people, as opposed to gratifying yourself artistically. Ministry is not about us and our wonderful talents. It's about people; it's about serving others. First Peter 4:10 discloses that each of us should use our gifts to serve others. If you focus on gratifying yourself artistically and forget all about ministering to people, ministry will be an empty experience. We artists spend so much time on technique and style that we often lose sight of the people we're trying to reach. When Jesus looked out on the crowds before him, his heart was moved with compassion (Matt. 9:36). He was sensitive to their needs because he was focused on people. Next time you're on the platform at church, try looking out at the people as Jesus would, with a heart full of compassion for each and every one of them.

We artists are fully capable of focusing compassionately on people, for we tend to be sensitive by nature. But when that sensitivity is turned inward on ourselves, we can become insensitive to the needs of others. We need to turn that wonderful sensitivity of ours outward to serve others. A good place to start being more aware of people's needs is with the artists with whom we serve at church. Galatians 5:13 tells us to "serve one another," and Romans 12:10 says to "be devoted to one another." We need to come to a meeting, a rehearsal, or a service ready and willing to serve. Instead of always asking, "What's in it for me?" or "What can I get out of this?" we need to ask, "How can I serve? What can I give?"

2. REMEMBER THAT THE MESSAGE IS MORE IMPORTANT

Keep in mind that the message is more important than the messenger. Paul was convinced that the effectiveness of his preaching depended not on how profound or persuasive he could be but on how much the Holy Spirit was allowed to work through him. That way the faith of his listeners would depend not on human wisdom but on the power of God (1 Cor. 2:4–5). Paul's words remind us that the purpose of our ministry, when we're ministering to God's people through the arts, is not to impress them with great art but to demonstrate God's power and love.

We can all tell, for example, when a singer is concentrating more on his or her vocal technique than on what they're singing. If taking out that lick that shows off your voice allows the lyric to come across more clearly, then take it out. Sometimes a simpler, uncluttered approach serves the message better. If you're an instrumentalist, this means that you play skillfully and with appropriate expression but don't draw undo attention to yourself. The platform at your church does not exist to advance your artistic ambitions. We need to serve the message, not ourselves.

By the way, if you're an instrumentalist, you might want to look at Psalm 68:25. In the worship service described here, the artists enter the sanctuary in a specific order. First there are the singers, followed by the instrumentalists, and then the dancers with tambourines. Charles Spurgeon points out that this order is no accident; it's by design. It represents the primacy of vocal music and the need for singers to be heard above the instruments. This is not to say that instrumental music is not important. I am primarily an instrumentalist. It simply serves to remind us of what every great instrumentalist already knows: they should not distract from or drown out the lyrics.[20] Instrumentalists should not compete with vocalists to be heard. We need to work together in serving the message of the song.

Whatever you do, don't do what Hezekiah did (2 Kings 20). When King Hezekiah became deathly ill, God not only promised that he would heal him but even made the sun regress six hours, from noon back to dawn, as a sign that Hezekiah would be healed. Emissaries from neighboring Babylon came to call on Hezekiah, because they saw the sun move backward and heard that God had done it on his behalf. The Babylonians were sun worshipers, so this was a great opportunity to give witness to the one true God. But instead Hezekiah took his guests up to the treasure room and proudly showed them all the kingdom's gold, silver, spices, oils, and armor. God had done this miraculous thing, and Hezekiah was showing off his personal trophy room. God's doing great things around us all the time. Let's not get stuck on how great we are, because it doesn't compare at all to God's greatness.

3. EXAMINE YOUR MOTIVATION

My fellow artists, what's your motivation for creating or performing? Is it to glorify God or to glorify yourself? Jeremiah's words are just as pertinent to us today as they were to the people of Israel: "Should you then seek great things for yourself? Do not seek them" (Jer. 45:5). If we're truly ministering in the name of Jesus, our motivation—what we are seeking—should be Christ Jesus and his glory, not our own. Jesus told us to seek first the kingdom of God, not the kingdom of self or the kingdom of art (Matt. 6:33). Christ is to have first place in everything we do (Col. 1:18). Remember what John the Baptist said? "He must become greater; I must become less" (John 3:30). That's the kind of attitude we need to have on the platform at all times. Paul says, "Whatever you do, do it all for the glory of God" (1 Cor. 10:31; see also Col. 3:17; 1 Peter 4:11). True ministry is motivated by a sincere desire for Jesus to be elevated, not us.

At one of the churches I served, we started a worship choir, so we scheduled an informational meeting for anyone interested in joining. Toward the end of the meeting, somebody asked me if this group was going to sing background all the time, or would they get to sing special numbers. My response was that in leading worship, we are all background. Jesus Christ is center stage, not us. He must increase and we must decrease. Worship is fundamentally a selfless task.

I'd like to add a word of caution regarding motives. I've seen artists get so vigilant about their motivation that they become obsessed with whether they're serving the Lord with a servant's heart. A friend of mine, a musician, admitted to me that he doesn't enjoy playing in church, because he's constantly worried that his motives are not right, that his inner motives are so well concealed he can't see them. That sounds to me like the work of the Accuser, the Evil One. The Bible says that Satan constantly tries to accuse us (Rev. 12:10). He loves to accuse us of wrong motives, even when we're on the platform, to get our focus off Jesus and onto ourselves. When Satan accuses, there is confusion. We wonder, *Is this from God or not?* But when God wants to deal with our motives, he does so in a loving, compassionate way (Isa. 42:3). His is not the voice of harsh accusation. His is that still, small voice like "a gentle whisper" (1 Kings 19:12) that tenderly convicts us of our sin and our need for him. So be careful not to become overly scrupulous about your motives. If the Lord is speaking to you about your motives, there will be no confusion or second-guessing. Instead there will be heartfelt conviction, with God gently bidding you to follow him and walk in his ways.

Every once in a while, someone will ask me if it's okay to feel confident on the platform. "Does that make me less humble?" they ask. A question like that usually comes from someone who equates humility with being spineless, apologetic, and wishy-washy. Second Timothy 1:7 says, "God has not given us a spirit of timidity, but of power and love and discipline" (NASB). That doesn't sound very spineless to me. If you acknowledge that your talent comes from God and give him the glory, it's okay to be confident that you can do what he's calling you to do.

4. DIE TO SELFISHNESS

I think every artist should memorize Philippians 2:3–4: "Do nothing out of selfish ambition or vain conceit. Rather, in humility value others above yourselves, not looking to your own interests but each of you to the interests of the others." I don't know how anyone can be a prima donna and have this verse sitting in their Bible. We need to die to selfishness and empty conceit and stop being so self-absorbed. First Corinthians 10:24 says, "No one should seek their own good, but the good of others." Real love does not seek its own (1 Cor. 13:5). Romans 12:10 says to "honor one another above yourselves." We need to regard everyone—other musicians on the team, other volunteers on the production crew, other artists at church—as more important than we are. This can be difficult for artists because of our tendency to be preoccupied with ourselves.

Throughout this book, I'll mention what I call my daily dangerous prayers. These are thoughts or Scripture verses that are so far from how I naturally think that I need to pray them into my heart and soul every day. They're dangerous prayers because they have the potential to radically change my life. One such verse is John 12:24: "Unless a kernel of wheat falls to the ground and dies, it remains only a single seed. But if it dies, it produces many seeds." Now, dying to self is not how I normally operate, so for a year and a half I prayed each day, "Lord, help me to die to self today. Show me how to apply this verse to my life today." Praying something like that every day made me realize how self-centered I really am.

For example, when I came home from work, I just wanted to veg because I was tired. But instead I was convicted to die to self and spend time with my wife, Sue, or play with my boys. In several relational conflicts, I was nudged by the Holy Spirit to die to being right all the time. And I was challenged time and again to die to the approval of others. I dare anyone to pray John 12:24 every day for a year and see if it doesn't change their life.

By way of caveat, this dying to self shouldn't be taken to the other extreme, in which we become doormats. Dying to self doesn't mean you abuse yourself or let yourself be abused. That's obviously not healthy, and many doormats can be just as self-absorbed as the next person, because they're proud of how lowly or humble they are.

No one is more important than anyone else (1 Cor. 12:20–25). That's why we need to look out for the interests of others instead of always trying to put our needs at the top of the agenda. This is the key to becoming a humble artist.

When Thomas à Kempis writes about the keys to inner peace, it sounds to me as if he's describing what it means to die to self.

> Endeavor, my son, rather to do the will
> of another than thine own.
> Choose always to have less rather than more.
> Seek always the lowest place, and to
> be inferior to every one.
> Wish always, and pray, that the will of
> God may be wholly fulfilled in thee.[21]

5. REMEMBER THAT MINISTRY IS A PRIVILEGE

Those of us who use our gifts in church need to remember that ministry is a privilege. God is in the business of bringing lost people to salvation. He could have sent angels to do the job (and maybe do it better), but instead he's entrusted us to make disciples of all the nations (Matt. 28:19).

Paul referred to ministry as a privilege and a high calling. He didn't take it for granted. He saw being "useful to the Master" (2 Tim. 2:21) as the most important thing you can do with your life. To Paul, being in ministry was a great honor and privilege.

Serving God is a way to honor him. It's our sacrifice of praise. What a testimony it is for a talented musician, actor, dancer, or artist to use his or her gifts in serving the Lord. What a wonderful example it is to our kids when they see Mom or Dad serving the Lord in some form of ministry. That parent is modeling what it means to serve God with the talents God gave him or her. That's the joy and reward of the Christian life. That's the great privilege of ministry. Proverbs 3:9 says to "honor the Lord with your wealth." Some of you have been given a wealth of talent. "From everyone who has been given much, much will be demanded" (Luke 12:48). Honor the Lord by serving him with your gifts and abilities.

Many of us have a strong desire to do something significant with our lives and our talents. We were created to do good works to the glory of God (Eph. 2:10). In Psalm 90:17, Moses asks God to "confirm" (NASB) the work of his hands. The margin of my Bible notes that a more literal translation would be "give permanence to" (NASB). Reading Moses' words prompted me to pray, "Lord, give permanence to the work of my hands; help me to do something meaningful and significant with my talent." Perhaps you resonate with that prayer and want to express to the Lord that same longing for significance.

Serving God can not only fulfill our desire for significance but also be extremely rewarding. We are merely "jars of clay" (2 Cor. 4:7), yet we carry the treasure of the good news of the gospel, God's plan of salvation, the hope of the world. It's an absolute privilege to be used of God. God not only rescued us from eternal damnation, he has blessed us and continues to bless us abundantly beyond what we deserve. Most of us feel that the very least we can do, after all he's done for us, is serve him with all our hearts.

David said, "What shall I return to the Lord for all his goodness to me?" (Ps. 116:12). Isaiah had a life-changing encounter with God, and he emerged from that saying, "Lord, I'm available. I'll do whatever you want. Here I am, send me!" (Isa. 6:8, my paraphrase). Really, what other response is there after you've tasted grace? We need to remember that it is not God who is lucky to have you and me in his service; we are the ones who are privileged to have a role, large or small, in advancing his kingdom.

The Difference between Volunteering and Being Called of God

Working with artists in the church, I've noticed a difference between those who volunteer out of obligation and those who sense a calling from God to serve. I'm not saying that volunteering is bad, and I'm not making a distinction between those who get paid and those who don't. In many churches no one is paid; everyone volunteers. So I'm not talking about whether one receives a paycheck. I'm referring instead to the attitude with which we serve and how we view our role in the church. I also don't mean to make a calling from God sound mysterious and otherworldly, like it's only for people who are called to be missionaries in Africa. I'm referring to the simple fact that we are called to steward the gifts God gives us, and one option for doing that is the church.

In 1 Chronicles 15:16–19, King David appoints musicians to lead the nation of Israel in worship. Thus they were appointed, or called, to serve. Colossians 4:17 says, "See to it that you complete the ministry you have *received in the Lord*" (my emphasis). In 1 Timothy 1:12, Paul says, "I thank Christ Jesus our Lord, who has given me strength, that he considered me trustworthy, appointing me to his service." Paul's ministry was not some routine act of volunteerism he did out of guilt or obligation. It was a special calling from God. Frederick Buechner said, "The place God calls you is the place where your deep gladness and the world's deep hunger meet."[22] For many artists serving in the church, life has taken on deeper meaning and significance because they're following the call God has put in their hearts.

Those who are called go about their ministry at church

differently than those engaged in mere volunteerism. Volunteers tend to put in minimum effort; they rarely do any outside practicing or preparation. But those who are called of God come to rehearsals and services as prepared as possible, because they want to offer God their best every time they lead his people in worship.[23] Volunteers are more prone to whine about what it costs to serve; they complain about having to get up early on Sunday morning for rehearsal or sound check. But artists responding to God's call are committed to serving. They want to be faithful stewards of the gifts God has given them, so they're dependable. They have good reason to get up early on Sunday, because they have something important to do.

Volunteers with a Calling

In distinguishing volunteers from those with a sense of calling, I want to be careful not to create two opposing camps and pit one against the other. We all start out volunteering, but for many of us, using our gifts at church is more than an extracurricular activity or hobby; it's a calling. We still might be unpaid volunteers, but we're heavily invested in the worship ministry at our church. God never intended ministry to be the responsibility of the chosen few who do full-time Christian work. God calls and equips believers to do the work of ministry (Eph. 4:11–12). Today, throughout the world, God is raising up an army of artistic volunteers in the church who are ministry-minded.

I remember being in a rehearsal with a drummer named Tony who was playing with us for the first time. During the rehearsal, I had to stop quite often to correct Tony or give him direction, so I was concerned about his being discouraged or feeling like I was picking on him. As soon as rehearsal ended, I made a beeline for Tony and asked him how he was doing. He sighed and then said, "I've been thinking about taking a few lessons, because there are a lot of new styles that I'm not up to date on right now. But I'm not giving up, because this is what God has called me to do." I smiled with amazement. Here was a man—a new Christian, by the way—who understood what it means to be called of God. He wasn't being paid to play drums at church. It was something God called him to do. That calling motivated him to persevere, even in situations that stretched his abilities.

I recall fondly another dear friend, Tim, who was a part of my ministry for years. Tim worked with computers, but he also played the trumpet at our church. Tim and I were in a small group together, and on one occasion he sought me out for career advice. He had just received an offer to work for another company, so he was trying to decide whether to take it. I asked him all sorts of questions about the company, his new position, the salary, and the benefits they were offering. But I could tell Tim was getting impatient with me. Finally, he interrupted and said, "Here's what I need to know from you. Do you think if I take this job I can still do all the things I'm doing at church?" Here was a man facing a career decision, and one of his chief concerns, in addition to how it would affect his family, was whether he could continue to fulfill his calling at church. My friend Tim understood that playing trumpet at church was not merely a diversion from a stressful job. God had given him a role to play in kingdom work, a sense of purpose, and he took it seriously. Both Tony and Tim exemplify what it means to be a ministry-minded artist who is called by God to use his or her talents at church.

Healthy Boundaries

Is it possible to serve too much? Can one overdo this serving thing? The answer is yes. You can spend too much time at church and neglect your family, your health, and even your relationship with the Lord. If you expect to serve the Lord for any length of time, you've got to set healthy boundaries. We all have to know how and when to say no, long before we reach personal crisis. The church has often been guilty of using and abusing artists. On the other hand, artists have sometimes played the martyr role and let themselves be used and abused.

Leaders often face a conundrum when it comes to scheduling artists for services. We don't want to burn out our team members, but at the same time, we don't want to deprive them of meaningful ministry opportunities. Over the years, I have erred on both sides. I have asked one too many times and it put someone over the edge. Then there were times when I tried to protect someone by not asking that person to sing or play, and I found out he or she was hurt because I didn't ask. I thought I was acting in their best interest, but it didn't turn out that way. If we could all work on setting healthy boundaries, leaders wouldn't need to second-guess or coerce, and artists would feel the freedom to say yes or no. When I offer someone with healthy boundaries a ministry opportunity and they say, "Thanks for asking, but I just can't do it this week," I don't feel bad for asking, and they don't feel bad for saying no.

There are seasons in church work that are naturally more demanding than others. Busy seasons come and go, and even though we can get weary in the middle of those busier seasons, they usually are short-lived. My family knows that Christmas and Easter are busy times for me. It's part of church work. But if I'm committed to having healthy boundaries and not overworking the rest of the year, Christmas and Easter or any other time of intense ministry become blips on the chart, exceptions to the rule instead of the norm. Scripture encourages us to be steadfast and not grow weary (1 Cor. 15:58; Gal. 6:10–11). We are also encouraged to give with a cheerful attitude, not under compulsion (2 Cor. 9:7), and to serve the Lord with joy and gladness (Ps. 100:2). The key to being faithful over the long haul and serving with a good attitude is setting healthy boundaries.

Serving an Audience of One

The ultimate test of servanthood is whether you can be content to serve an audience of one, when it's okay to serve in anonymity, when you can throw yourself into a bit part, when you no longer live for the approval of others, when the size of your audience doesn't matter anymore, and when the size of the role you play is less important than being faithful and obedient. Serving an audience of one can be challenging, because we tend to love the approval of others more than God's approval (John 12:43). We seek the favor of those around us instead of the favor of God (Gal. 1:10). We want to be noticed. Jesus warns against that motivation (Matt. 6:1). When you no longer crave the spotlight, when you don't need to be noticed or recognized, and when you're not above doing grunt work such as stacking chairs, you're on your way to being the selfless servant God really uses.

Philip Yancey compares serving an audience of one to a stained-glass window. "Tensions and anxieties flame within me the moment I forget I am living my life for the one-man audience of Christ and slip into living my life to assert myself in a competitive world. Previously, my main motivation in life was to do a painting of myself, filled with bright colors and profound insights, so that all who looked upon it would be impressed. Now, however, I find that my role is to be a mirror, to brightly reflect the image of God through me. Or perhaps the metaphor of stained glass would serve better, for, after all, God will illumine through my personality and body."[24]

Artists who create or perform to serve an audience of one are people of godly character, meaning that God's character is revealed in them and through them.

In my early years, I was discipled by a man who became a treasured friend. His name is John Allen. I learned all about servanthood from John, not because we ever did a Bible study on it but because he lived with a servant's heart toward all people. John is a handyman (and I am not). He would come over to our house and fix broken water heaters, leaky pipes, and dilapidated drywall. He'd come over and help with yard work, because to John it was a chance to serve and to spend time with me, talking about the Lord. When I faced major decisions in my life, he offered not only to pray for me but to fast as long as I was fasting, to see if God would confirm his will through both of us. That's a real servant. John earned a modest music teacher's salary, yet he shared his financial resources freely and cheerfully whenever a brother or a sister was in need. He was always there when I needed him, always asking, "What can I do to help?" I have since moved several states away from my friend, but I will never forget the impact of watching someone live out the heart of a servant right before my eyes. John showed me what true servanthood is. He showed me what it is like to be overjoyed to serve an audience of one.

Follow-Up Questions for Group Discussion

1. What do you think Jesus, as the prime example of servanthood, would be like at rehearsal?
2. What do you think Jesus would be like on the platform leading worship?
3. Can you think of someone in your life who's been a positive example of servanthood? What is it about him or her that stands out in your mind?
4. Where would you put yourself on the humility continuum? With empty conceit on one end and false humility on the other, which end of the spectrum do you lean toward?
5. What does servanthood look like in your ministry?
6. What kinds of things keep artists from being able to serve an audience of one?
7. Why, in your opinion, is it difficult for artists to have healthy boundaries when it comes to their work?

8. How can an artist be a confident person and still have a servant's heart?

PERSONAL ACTION STEPS

1. Offer your gifts to God. If you've never thanked the Lord for the gifts and talents he's given you, do so and tell him you're committed to using your gifts not as you please but as he wills. If you really want to make your commitment special, express it artistically in some way.
2. Offer your gifts to the church. Paul saw himself as a servant to the church for Jesus Christ (2 Cor. 4:5). Express to your ministry leader or pastor, either verbally or in writing, your commitment to serve the people of your church with your gifts and talents.
3. If you've offended anybody by your lack of true humility, acknowledge your sin to whomever it affected and ask that person for forgiveness.
4. Determine whether you have healthy boundaries in serving. If not, decide what it would take for you to have healthier boundaries and begin making those changes. Choose someone to whom you can be accountable regarding this.
5. Galatians 5:13 exhorts us to serve one another out of love. Identify someone whom you can serve in a kind and loving way this week and decide how to do that.

CHAPTER 3

THE ARTIST IN COMMUNITY

THE SCENE: EMILY HAS JUST ARRIVED home after a long and grueling rehearsal at church. It is late. Before she can get out of the car, her phone rings. She rummages through her purse to find it. Emily is the creative arts director at Lakeview Church. For several weeks now she's been throwing herself into rehearsals for Holy Week services, which begin this Sunday. As she pulls out her phone, she assumes that, like everything else in her life these days, this call has something to do with church. On the line is Jacob from the video team.

> **JACOB:** *(sounding urgent)* Uh, Emily? I hate to call you at home, and I'm sorry for calling so late. Are you busy?
>
> **EMILY:** *(smiling)* Well, I'm not quite home yet. I just

pulled into the garage, so I'm still in the car. I guess I can talk. You sound troubled, Jacob. Are you okay?

JACOB: Well . . . um . . . no. I hate to bring this up. I know how busy you are, but there's a lot of people in the worship ministry who are up in arms right now. I don't know if you know how bad it is. After rehearsal, I was talking with Paul, and he's really upset.

EMILY: I'm sorry to hear that. What is he upset about?

JACOB: He feels like if he were to quit the team, no one would care. And some of us have been talking and everybody feels the same way.

EMILY: You mean like if you left the team, no one would notice or care?

JACOB: Yeah. No one really feels connected.

EMILY: How long has Paul been upset? When I spoke with him tonight, he seemed okay. He didn't act like he was upset. And he certainly didn't mention anything about it.

JACOB: Well, I'm not surprised. He's pretty confused right now. He doesn't think you like him.

EMILY: Really? I'm sorry to hear that. I like Paul very much.

JACOB: Well, he's so upset he's thinking about leaving the church. That's how angry he is.

EMILY: Is he mad at me?

JACOB: Well . . . yeah. He's still angry that he didn't get the tech director position.

EMILY: Wow, that was three years ago.

JACOB: I know, but he really had his heart set on leading our team. I understand why you hired Frank. Frank's new and younger, but Paul's got way more experience.

EMILY: Now that you mention it, I thought it was odd that Paul suddenly left the room when the cast sang "Happy Birthday" to Frank tonight.

JACOB: Well, yeah, I think Paul was hurt by that, especially since no one wished him a happy birthday last week.

EMILY: I see. But I don't think anyone knew it was his birthday—

JACOB: *(interrupting angrily)* That's the point! We talk about fellowship and community all the time around here, but it's all just talk. We're not a team at all. What's happening to Paul happens all the time. You expect to see this kind of thing out in the world, certainly not in the church! Aren't we supposed to love and care for each other? No wonder Paul's hurt. I would be too!

EMILY: Jacob, did you tell Paul to come and talk to me?

JACOB: Oh no, he can't do that. A lot of people are very intimidated by you, and besides we all know how busy you are.

EMILY: But you're putting yourself in the middle of something that's really between me and Paul.

JACOB: Oh, we haven't been gossiping or anything. Paul just needs to vent, and I'm just there to listen. But the more I hear what he's saying, the more angry I get that one of our faithful members who's been around a long time is being shoved aside.

EMILY: Well, I certainly don't want Paul to feel like he's being shoved aside. I really wish he would come and talk to me. It sounds like he's feeling insecure and wants to know where he stands with me. It is disappointing to hear this secondhand—

JACOB: *(interrupting)* Um, Emily, I've got another call coming in. Sorry, I need to run.

EMILY: *(slowly)* Okay . . . Thanks for calling, Jacob. I'll see you tomorrow night at rehearsal.

Emily resists the urge to throw her cell phone out the window. At this late hour, she doesn't have the energy. Instead she gets out of her car, trudges up the walkway, steps into her apartment, and plops down on the bed, exhausted. She braces herself for another sleepless night.

Questions for Group Discussion

1. What do you appreciate most about the team you're serving on in your church (the choir, the worship team, the vocal team, the band or orchestra, the dance team, the sound, video, or lighting team, the visual arts team)?
2. In our opening scenario, Jacob suggests that a lot of people are upset and everybody feels a certain way. Do you think statements like that are blown out of proportion, or could they be true?
3. Do you think it was healthy for Paul to vent his anger and frustration with Jacob? Why or why not?
4. In your opinion, what are some of the advantages to doing ministry in teams?
5. What are some of the challenges of doing ministry in teams?
6. If Satan wanted to undermine the unity of your team, how might he go about it?
7. Have you ever been on a successful team of any kind (an athletic team, a team of workers, a music group, a drama or dance club)? What made that team successful?

The Church as a Colony of Artists

I've always been fascinated by the colonies of artists that form around major artistic movements. My favorite example is Paris in the early 1900s, where artists congregated and fed off each other's creativity and ideas. At that time, exciting innovations were taking place in the arts. Composers, visual artists, dancers, choreographers, authors, and poets all mixed and mingled in a beehive of artistic activity. My favorite composer, Igor Stravinsky, was part of this historic colony of artists, and his circle of friends included fellow composers Claude Debussy, Maurice Ravel, Erik Satie, and Manuel de Falla. It was a time when the arts overlapped in exciting ways as Stravinsky rubbed shoulders with artists like Pablo Picasso, Henri Matisse, and Jean Cocteau. This group wasn't without its disagreements and jealousies, but many of these artists were friends. They'd go to concerts and art galleries together. They'd get together at each other's homes and talk long into the night about music, art, and literature. On one occasion, Stravinsky sat down with Debussy at the piano and they played through a transcription of an orchestral piece Stravinsky was developing. It just happened to be *The Rite of Spring*, one of the landmark masterpieces of the twentieth century. Imagine being a fly on the wall and overhearing that conversation! These artists changed the world with their art. All the great new work at that time was coming out of

Paris, and artists from all over the world were flocking there to study. Paris in the early 1900s was an exciting place to be. The arts were thriving and artists were flourishing.

Many Christian artists long to be in a place where the arts are flourishing, where God is using artistic expression in a powerful way. We yearn for a place where we can connect in meaningful ways with other artists, a place where we can learn from one another and cheer each other on. I believe that's part of what God wants our churches to be: communities that harness the arts for God's glory and nurture artists.

The sense of teamwork and camaraderie that those Parisian artists shared in the early 1900s intrigues me because artists don't always work well together, nor do they always get along with each other. Many of us are more introverted by nature; we're lone rangers. In a book titled *The Musical Temperament*, author Anthony Kemp states that while many "musicians are distinctly introverted, there is also a 'boldness' which arises not only from their considerable inner strengths but also from their sense of independence. Musicians tend to share these qualities with several other creative types."[25]

Getting artists who are introverted and independent to function as a team is no easy task. Like many artists who are thrown together with others on a team, Igor Stravinsky had to learn how to function as a team player. Howard Gardner, in his book *Creating Minds*, points out that when Stravinsky was asked to join the Ballets Russes, it changed his life overnight. "Stravinsky became a valued member of what was possibly the most innovative performing artistic group in the world. . . . Now instead of working mostly alone, Stravinsky had almost daily intercourse with the ensemble . . . set designers, dancers, choreographers, and even those responsible for the business end of the enterprise."[26] Stepping out of his comfort zone and embracing life in community with other artists made Stravinsky an even greater, more well-rounded composer.

Relationships Matter

Many artists spend a great deal of time working alone; we practice or create by ourselves. At some point, though, we usually end up working with other artists. Even if you don't consider yourself to be very relational, you need to learn how to relate to and get along with other artists. Even if you're extremely introverted, you're deceived if you think you can live a meaningful existence isolated from others or live the Christian life apart from other believers. To know and be known is a basic human need. We can't be lone rangers. We need fellowship. We need each other.

Many years ago, an incident occurred that forever changed my view of the importance of relationships in my life. I had an appendectomy that involved some complications and the need for two surgeries. I was in and out of the hospital for two weeks, and it took me three months to fully recover. That was a dark time for me. I remember feeling so lonely in my hospital room that I cried every time Sue and the boys (who were very young at the time) left. I found myself eagerly looking forward to visits from friends, relatives, anybody.

I can only imagine how lonely it must be for people who are homebound. My long convalescence made me realize that I had taken too many relationships for granted. You really don't know what you've got till it's gone. I realized that relationships were not as much of a priority for me as they should have been. I was too busy for people. I wasn't doing anything to initiate new friendships or build the ones I already had.

When I got out of the hospital, I was determined to change all that, and I adopted a new motto: Relationships matter. Instead of working through lunch, I tried to find someone to eat with. I opened up larger blocks of time to allow for more personal appointments. Instead of waiting for people to call me, I started calling them, and I became more proactive about spending time with people.

Relationships are a lot of work. They don't happen overnight; they need to be cultivated. Even those friendships that seem to happen accidentally, when people are thrown together by circumstance, involve work. Some of the people who complain the loudest about not having any friends are the same people who don't work at having meaningful relationships. If you want to have quality relationships, you have to put in the effort.

My best friend lives a thousand miles away. We go back a long way and have a lot of history together. Ours is the kind of friendship in which, even if we haven't talked in a while, it's easy to pick up where we left off. He's someone to whom I can tell my darkest secrets. It would be a shame to let that friendship die, but it's a lot of work, especially because we live so far apart. I'm now convinced that the time I've invested in this and all my other friendships is time well spent, because relationships matter.

Teamwork

Church work has convinced me that ministry is best done in teams. The beauty of working in teams is that together we can accomplish greater things for God. We come together to do what no one of us could do alone. With all of us pitching in and pulling in the same direction, we reap huge dividends.

When you're part of a ministry team, you have a sense of belonging. You have a place on the team—you belong with these people—for two reasons.

1. *Your gifts and abilities have created a niche for you on the team.* Proverbs 22:29 says that a person who is talented and works hard will go far. Because you're

talented and work hard, you've been invited to serve in ministry. Your gifts and abilities have made room for you on the team. You share the same calling as others who have been entrusted with an artistic talent. As a result, you play an important role not only as a member of your ministry team but also as part of a worldwide community of Christian artists!

2. *Your personality has created a place for you on the team.* First Corinthians 12:18 says that God "placed the parts in the body, every one of them, just as he wanted them to be." When God calls you to be part of a team, he takes into account who you are as well as what you can do. No one is going to contribute to the cause and community of the team in the same way that you do. Even someone who has the same talents and gift mix that you have won't contribute exactly as you do, because you're two different people with two different personalities. You're not indispensable but you are irreplaceable.

Things That Hinder Teamwork

In spite of how powerful and meaningful team ministry can be, the task of getting a group of artists to function as a team is a difficult one. A worship arts director informed me that his pastor shut down their church choir because there was so much arguing among members. A young worship leader shared that at his church not a rehearsal went by without someone blowing up at someone else. Bickering and backstabbing had become normal occurrences.

The Evil One does everything he can to disrupt teams. He tries to sow disunity, undermine morale, and frustrate even the simplest of plans. Satan does his utmost to bring down any and every team that's devoted to advancing the kingdom of God. Let's analyze briefly the four main causes of team dysfunction.

I. SELFISHNESS

Selfishness is the biggest obstacle for any team to overcome. There's no way a team can function effectively if its members constantly put themselves and their needs ahead of everyone else. People who are focused only on themselves will miss the big picture. This was the problem with the Prodigal Son's brother (Luke 15:11–32). Instead of celebrating his wayward brother's homecoming with the rest of his family, this young man allowed his self-centeredness to make him resentful. It caused him to miss the more important thing: his lost brother was saved.

We can get so focused on ourselves that we miss what's really important. That's me-first thinking. When we're angry because we didn't get to sing the solo we think we deserve or when we manipulate conversations to focus on ourselves, that's me-first thinking. When the team is celebrating a recent success and we're pouting in the corner because we didn't get to play the role we wanted to play, that's a me-first mindset.

2. GRUMBLING AND COMPLAINING

Grumbling and complaining are usually the result of selfishness. Have you ever noticed how much we complain? We complain about the weather. We complain about our jobs. We complain about the government. We complain about our sports teams. Complaining seems to be human nature. The people of Israel grumbled against Moses all the time (Ex. 15:24; Num. 16:41; 17:5). Many of us with artistic temperaments tend to complain and grumble whenever things don't go our way.

I received an email from a worship pastor who quit his job because he could no longer put up with "all the whininess and apathy." Satan had sabotaged this church's worship team by getting all the musicians to be negative. Philippians 2:14 instructs us to "do everything without grumbling or arguing," both of which can sow the kind of discord that cripples teams and splits churches.

3. A COMPETITIVE SPIRIT

Healthy competition can bring out the best in us. The upside of competition in the arts, as in athletics, is that it can spur us on to grow as artists. The downside is that competition can ruin team morale. When people stop rooting for each other and refuse to cheer each other on because they're constantly competing with one another, they will never function as a team. Instead of competing, we need to learn to cooperate.

4. DISUNITY

John 17 records one of Jesus' last prayers before he died on the cross. Of all the things he could have prayed for, utmost in his mind was the unity of the disciples. He prayed for them to be one (vv. 21–22) and to be "brought to complete unity" (v. 23). Unity is important to God, and it's not something to be taken lightly. Scripture instructs us to "make every effort to keep the unity of the Spirit through the bond of peace" (Eph. 4:3). If each team member owns the responsibility for team unity, that team will be "like-minded, having the same love, being one in spirit and of one mind" (Phil. 2:2). Psalm 133:1 exclaims, "How good and pleasant it is when God's people live together in unity!"

When Solomon dedicated the temple, the priests and musicians came forth "regardless of their divisions" (2 Chron. 5:11). They all checked their egos at the door and stood before God not according to status or rank but unified as God's people. They had a powerful worship time at this ceremony, and the arts played a major role (vv. 12–13). This passage also shows us that unity is a powerful testimony to the presence of God. God's presence was so strong at this dedication that people were falling down. It all started with the people being unified. Don't ever think unity is optional. It's required if we're going to do anything together in God's name.

Christian unity is a powerful witness to unchurched people. If there were a colony of Christ-honoring artists who got along with each other and truly loved each other, the world would sit up and take notice, because that doesn't happen among artists in the entertainment industry. For years I conducted a church orchestra, and I used to tell my players that they were the most visible example of team unity in the entire church. We were a diverse collection of ages, ethnic groups, abilities, and backgrounds, but we all had to learn to play together and get along. The unity of our worship teams might prove to be a more powerful testimony than our music.

Team Values

Every team has core values, written or unwritten, spoken or unspoken, that set the standard of behavior for that team. This code of values defines what's acceptable conduct and what isn't. It says in effect, "This is how we do things on this team." When you're part of a team, you adhere to certain expectations, requirements, and rules.

For years I worked at a church where every staff member was expected to keep his or her office neat and tidy. My first day on the job, I was working feverishly all day to prepare music for rehearsal that evening. I didn't take a break, hardly ate, and worked right up to the start of rehearsal, which went long. By the time it was all over, I had music strewn about my office, and papers, folders, and unopened mail piled high on my desk. I thought about cleaning up before I left, but it was late and I was exhausted. Besides, I could do it first thing in the morning. So I thought. The next morning someone from building services greeted me at my office door. He was very polite but firm. "I noticed you left your office in quite a mess last night," he began. "I know you're new, but I just want you to know that we don't do things like that around here. We keep our offices neat and clean." I thought about explaining to this fine gentleman that I was an artist and shouldn't be expected to conform to cultural norms, but somehow I didn't think he'd buy it. Needless to say, I kept a very orderly office from that day on.

A team's core values reflect its priorities. If rehearsal is a priority, then every team member should try to attend. If punctuality is an important value, then everyone should make an effort to show up on time. A friend of mine who is a high school band director sent me a list of core values he put together for his band. If you were to play in my friend's band, this is what would be expected of you:

1. Be on time for rehearsals.
2. Be ready to perform in all aspects (warmed up, instrument mechanically set, all equipment available).
3. Take care of your instrument.
4. Bring a pencil to rehearsal.
5. Listen to the conductor.
6. Mark your music—do not trust memory to skip an ending, take a repeat, etc.
7. Constantly listen and adjust pitch and volume while playing.
8. Be ready for entrances.
9. Sincerely attempt to play the part correctly.
10. Play second or third part with as much enthusiasm as first part.
11. Practice music between rehearsals and continually strive to improve.
12. Interpret as the conductor wishes.
13. Do not miss rehearsals.

By laying out expectations for all team members, a code of priorities reflects and perpetuates a certain kind of culture that enables a team to function at maximum capacity.

A team's core values not only need to be established but also must be articulated so everyone understands what's expected of them. I used to get angry when anyone arrived late for rehearsal, especially when they acted like it was no big deal. I'd be fuming inside and indignant that anybody could be so nonchalant. Then I realized I had never communicated that punctuality was an important value to me. In my book, punctuality is a basic human courtesy; it's disrespectful to waste other people's time by making them wait. Once my musicians heard my view on the matter, they made an effort to show up on time for rehearsal. Or when they couldn't help being late, they either alerted me ahead of time or explained why they were late when they arrived.

Being on a team demands that all participants adjust to comply with their group's expectations. I have a friend who was habitually late to meetings and rehearsals at church. He had the same problem at work, by the way. Since this man was part of a team that valued punctuality, he decided that if he walked in and the meeting or rehearsal had already started, he would apologize to everyone he had kept waiting. Having to say, "I'm sorry" every time he was late eventually broke my friend of this bad habit. He was even more prompt for meetings at work. Whatever changes you need to make to accommodate your team's values and priorities will probably pay off in other areas of your life as well.

What Does It Mean to Be a Team Player?

A team's core values are specific to that group, but there are some basic responsibilities that define what it means for an artist in the church to be a team player. Most of what I know about being a team player I learned through either music or athletics. In sports there are certain things you do for the sake of the team. My son's Little League coach told the boys to throw and run every day because it's good for them and good for the team. So my son practiced those disciplines, knowing it was part of his responsibility to the team.

If you're part of a team of artists, there are certain things you need to do for the sake of the team. The success of your ministry depends on each member understanding what it means to be a team player.

I. A TEAM PLAYER IS COMMITTED TO THE MISSION

In ministry being committed to the cause of the team means that we put the church's mission above our own agenda. From time to time, I hear stories about arts ministries in which the team members aren't all on the same page. The result is musicians, tech people, and choir members all doing their own thing instead of coming together for the common good. A musician who pushes a favorite style of music even though it doesn't fit the occasion is putting his or her own agenda ahead of the team's. Philippians 2:2 tells us to be "like-minded, having the same love, being one in spirit and of one mind." When everyone on a team is intent on the same purpose, that team will do great things for God.

In Chicago, where I served, we were fortunate to

have the greatest player in the history of basketball playing for the Bulls. I think what was most impressive about Michael Jordan was the example he set of a team player. On December 17, 1996, the Chicago Bulls were playing the Los Angeles Lakers, and Jordan was having what for him was an off night. (We later found out that he was battling the flu.) Coach Phil Jackson asked Michael to be a decoy. "We saw Michael was struggling in the third quarter, and I told him to be a decoy and hit the other guys," Jackson said to reporters after the game. Imagine that: asking the greatest player who's ever played the game to be a decoy, to put the team ahead of his ego and agenda. Did Michael do it? Yes. After the game, Coach Jackson said, "Michael did a great job of playing the role and hitting the open man." Did it work? Yes. The Bulls won 129–123 in overtime. In addition to being an elite basketball player, Michael Jordan was also a great team player who put his team's mission to win games ahead of his agenda.

Sometimes last-minute changes are suggested for a service. Sometimes a song that someone's put a lot of work into gets cut. Are you flexible when that happens, or does it make you angry and resentful? Are you more committed to your agenda than to the cause? Dealing with changes, large and small, is always a good test of character.

In the Old Testament, Amasai, a leader in King David's army, speaks on behalf of his fellow soldiers and says to their commander in chief, "We are yours, David! We are with you, son of Jesse! Success, success to you, and success to those who help you, for your God will help you" (1 Chron. 12:18). Amasai assures David that he and his men are behind him all the way. They believe in a common cause and remain committed to their mission. Does your ministry leader know you're committed to the team? When was the last time you told your leader as much? Do you stand behind the team, its leader, and its cause? Do you put the team's mission ahead of your agenda?

2. A TEAM PLAYER ENCOURAGES TEAMMATES

For the church to nurture artists, leaders need to cultivate an environment that is encouraging, life-giving, and supportive. Most of us have no difficulty encouraging someone whose gifts and abilities pose no threat to our place in the ministry. A sign of godly character is a willingness to root for and rejoice in the success of those with talents similar to our own. First Corinthians 12:26 says, "If one member is honored, all the members rejoice with it" (NASB). Can you pull for someone who's been given the opportunity, the solo, the part, or the recognition that you wanted?

In the entertainment world, it's unheard of for artists to encourage one another. It's a fiercely competitive and cutthroat business. Someone with talents that overlap yours is looked upon as a threat. This should not be so in the church. Instead of competing, we need to cooperate with each other, to "encourage one another and build each other up" (1 Thess. 5:11). I love seeing a veteran singer applaud the efforts of a new vocalist on the team, or an instrumentalist cheering on a fellow band member. Proverbs 3:27 implores us not to "withhold good from those to whom it is due." All artists need encouragement, and it's wrong for us to withhold support from one another. Is there anybody on your team at church whom you need to encourage this week?

3. A TEAM PLAYER DOESN'T CARE WHO GETS THE CREDIT

Michelangelo overheard a group of tourists in Saint Peter's Basilica observing his famous *Pieta*, the marble sculpture of Mary holding the crucified Jesus across her lap. The tourists were trying to figure out who the artist was. After hearing them attribute his work to other sculptors, Michelangelo returned in the middle of the night and across the band wrapped around Mary, in big, bold letters, he carved, "Michelangelo Buonarroti of Florence made this." It was the only work he ever signed.

Like Michelangelo, we artists in the church can become indignant if our efforts are not recognized or acknowledged. We may even feel taken for granted and unappreciated. Of course, our efforts never go unnoticed by God. He sees, appreciates, and rewards (Matt. 6:4, 6, 18). Yet we still bristle when our efforts get overlooked by others. A wise man once said, "It is amazing how much can be accomplished if no one cares who gets the credit." If you really believe in the cause of your team, does it matter who gets the credit? If a mission is accomplished, does everyone need to know how much of it was your doing?

King David wanted to build a temple for God, but God rejected his proposal and instead chose David's son, Solomon, to build it. Someone else—not David—would oversee this monumental construction project and get all the credit and glory. The great edifice wouldn't even bear David's name; it would eventually be called Solomon's Temple. And it was David's idea in the first place! So how did David respond? Instead of sulking or getting angry or going the passive-aggressive route and undermining his son's efforts, David got behind the project as best he could. He helped gather the materials needed for construction, he gave financially, and he did all this with a great attitude (1 Chronicles 22; 29:2–3). He pitched in and did whatever he could because building the temple was more important than who did it. That's a team player!

4. A TEAM PLAYER BRINGS ALL SPIRITUAL GIFTS TO THE TABLE

I've seen too many artists focus solely on their talent and neglect their spiritual gifts.[27] They create or perform and that's it. What about an artist who also has the gift of mercy, encouragement, service, shepherding, or evangelism? The team can't function optimally without these spiritual skills. First Corinthians 14:26 paints a beautiful picture of these gifts in action: "When you come together, each of you has a hymn, or a word of instruction, a revelation, a tongue or an interpretation. Everything must be done so that the church may be built up." While your spiritual gift may or may not factor into every worship service, it can certainly play a key role in the life of your team.

Convinced that spiritual gifts are given to strengthen and edify others, team players bring those gifts to every team gathering. They attend rehearsal not just to learn the music but also to minister to their fellow artists. Someone with the gift of encouragement could come to rehearsal looking for a teammate who's struggling and pray for them or encourage them. Hebrews 10:24 tells us to "consider how we may spur one another on toward love and good deeds." Meetings, rehearsals, setting up the stage, and teardown can become opportunities for teammates to minister to one another. Next time you're driving to church, ask yourself, "How can I use my spiritual gift today to stimulate my brothers and sisters in Christ to do good things for God? How can I build up my teammates?"

5. A TEAM PLAYER IS COMMITTED TO RESOLVING RELATIONAL CONFLICT

Resolving relational conflict in a biblical way plays a key role in maintaining team unity. In his letter to the Philippians,

Paul calls out two women at the church who are at odds with each other and begs them to work out their differences and come to mutual agreement (Phil. 4:2). Relational strife doesn't bother me as a leader, because conflict is inevitable when you're trying to build community. What does concern me, though, is that we resolve all relational discord in a biblical way.

In Matthew 18, Jesus outlines a procedure for conflict resolution. The first step is to go directly to the person with whom you're at odds and talk it out (v. 15). I know it's not easy to approach someone who's hurt us; we'd rather avoid confrontation. But when this is done right, the relationship is not only restored, it's deepened. One conversation might be all it takes to resolve the conflict, but sometimes it takes several meetings. If the two of you can't resolve the issue on your own, pull in one or two mature brothers or sisters who can help mediate (v. 16). If that doesn't do the trick, bring in the elders or other church staff to help sort out your differences (v. 17).[28]

It's wrong for team members to ignore Jesus' words and not go directly to the person who offended them and talk. It's not right to triangulate—to talk to others about the problem we're having with so-and-so but never go straight to the source. If we haven't gone directly to the person with whom we're in conflict, we have no business going to anyone else and poisoning his or her opinion of that person. Proverbs 17:9 tells us that someone who gossips and slanders or tries to play the middleman can ruin even the best of friendships. This also pertains to conflicts that team members have with team leaders. If you have a problem with your ministry director or you're unhappy with how things are going for you on the team, go directly to that leader instead of talking behind his or her back.

Early in my ministry, I had an experience that solidified for me the importance of resolving relational disputes. I had two musicians on the team who were constantly sniping at each other. They didn't get along at all; at every rehearsal the air was thick with tension. I observed this for a few weeks and realized that their deep hostility was not going away by itself. Meanwhile it was becoming noticeable to everyone else, and it was hurting the morale of our team. I pulled both members aside and encouraged them to resolve their issues in the manner laid out in Matthew 18, then sat back and watched for a couple more weeks. But there was no movement on either part, so I had to do something.

The following Sunday I approached them individually during sound check and asked them to meet me in my office after the service. You can imagine their surprise when they realized they were meeting not only me but each other as well. And it got even more uncomfortable from there because I left the room. But before departing, I explained that I had been after them for two weeks to resolve their conflict according to Matthew 18 but had seen no effort on their part to do so.

"I am going to leave now," I said, "and I don't care how many meetings it takes, but you two are going to start today to talk this thing out." And I left. I don't know how long they sat in silence before any conversation began, but when I came back, the two of them were talking. By the end, they both had expressed their anger and apologized, and from then on they enjoyed an amicable relationship.

Both individuals admitted to me later that until this incident they had never experienced a biblical approach to conflict resolution. They had never even seen it modeled. They both grew up in homes where family members dealt with conflict by yelling, screaming, slamming doors, and giving one another the cold shoulder. This was the first time they had followed Jesus' approach to resolving differences. Sadly, many people, including those from Christian homes, can identify with that predicament. Your team—your church family—is an ideal place to learn how to resolve relational conflict in a healthy way.

The Story of a Successful Team of Artists

The Old Testament features an inspiring story of a group of artists who accomplished something great for God. In Exodus 35 Moses rallied the people of Israel to build the tabernacle. Then he called the artists together, divided them into teams, and gave them their assignments. There was great attention to detail; the Bible devotes four chapters to describing the artistry that went into erecting the tabernacle. When it was all done, a cloud representing God's majesty rested over them, and the divine glory filled the tabernacle (Ex. 40:34). Can you imagine how those artists felt? They combined their efforts, worked hard, and functioned as a team. The Lord anointed their efforts and blessed their work. They came together to do something that no one of them could have done alone. May you too experience the joy and reward of being part of a community of artists that's dedicated to serving the Lord.

Follow-Up Questions for Group Discussion

1. Can you think of something your team has done recently that would be an example of coming together to do what no one of you could do alone?
2. How can you use your spiritual gift at rehearsals or meetings?
3. How can you encourage or bless someone on your team this week?
4. What spiritual gifts are represented by members of your team? How can those gifts contribute to your team's overall success?
5. It has been said that fellowship, or community, is the art of knowing and being known. Are you better at one than the other, or are you pretty good at both? Explain.

6. Which of the five characteristics of a team player, listed in this chapter, represents an area of needed growth in your life? Make a commitment to the Lord, to your team, or to your leader to grow in that area.

7. How can your team become even more effective in ministry this next year?

PERSONAL ACTION STEPS

1. Get your team together and come up with a list of values that captures the characteristics or behavior of an effective team member. To begin, you could write at the top of a flip chart, “This is the way we do things on the [insert name, i.e., worship] team” and pool together everyone’s ideas.

2. Define specifically your role on the team. Considering not only your talent but also your spiritual gifts and personality, determine what you uniquely bring to the team.

3. Is there anyone on the team now with whom you are in conflict? If so, go to that person and take steps to resolve the issue.

4. If there are any conflicts or lingering bad feelings in your relationship with your ministry director, go to him or her and take steps to clear the air.

5. Offer words of support to someone on your team who is struggling.

CHAPTER 4

EXCELLENCE VERSUS PERFECTIONISM

ELLEN STARTED PLAYING THE VIOLIN WHEN she was only four years old, and she showed a great deal of promise throughout her early years. She improved at a rapid pace because she loved to practice. When other girls her age were playing dress up, Ellen was playing Mozart. One of her earliest childhood memories was hearing a local performance of Beethoven's Ninth Symphony. As soon as the orchestra started to play, she cried. She was mesmerized by the different sounds of the orchestra and held spellbound by the violin section. Ellen loved the violin and she loved music.

Ellen also loved church. Her parents were Christians and very involved at their church. When she was eight years old, Ellen accepted Jesus Christ as her personal Savior. She even played a few violin solos in church and enjoyed doing that very much. But Ellen's big dream was to perform as a soloist with the world's major orchestras and record her favorite violin concertos. She felt that was what God wanted her to do with her life. She won a scholarship to attend a reputable music conservatory. The competition at the conservatory was fierce, and though it was disheartening at first, Ellen realized she wasn't good enough to pursue a solo career, so she set her sights on performing as a member of a major orchestra. She graduated and went from audition to audition, trying to land a job in the string section of an orchestra. It didn't happen. She became discouraged. Concluding that she wasn't cut out for playing professionally, Ellen decided to teach violin lessons. She started teaching privately, going to students' homes, and it was rough going at first as she struggled to build up a clientele, but after a few short years she had a thriving teaching business.

Ellen met and married Tom, a fine Christian man. They bought a house and set Ellen up to teach in their home. At this time, they began to attend a nearby church, and Ellen began to play at worship services. When they started having kids, Ellen had to cut back on teaching, but she still played for church. At first it was a great outlet for her, a refreshing break from teaching. She liked the church and she liked the people. She was often asked to play solos, which she enjoyed doing. But as time went on, Ellen became more and more unhappy with her playing because it didn't sound like it did in college, when she was practicing eight hours a day. Yet as the mother of two toddlers, she barely had time to practice.

Ellen grew increasingly disappointed in herself. She had high standards and great expectations, and she couldn't bear the thought of falling short. She came to rehearsal discouraged and left defeated. She had a difficult time receiving compliments. People at church told her they loved her playing, but Ellen would be thinking about that one song that she wished had gone better or that one note that was out of tune. She had a hard time letting go of things like that. Her mistakes and shortcomings loomed large in her mind, and she was haunted by them.

Ellen's frustration built to such an intensity that she decided to quit playing her violin. Although she missed playing at church, she didn't miss the negative thoughts about herself that came with it. Ellen was in turmoil. Music had been a source of joy to her. She used to love music, but now she hated it because it constantly reminded her that she didn't measure up.

Ellen felt God must be disappointed in her too. She felt guilty that she wasn't using her talent, but she was angry at God. Why didn't he give her a solo career or a job in an orchestra? How come things never worked out for her? If God wanted her to play the violin, why was her musical experience always so frustrating?

Ellen continued to teach, but even her teaching suffered because Ellen just wasn't quite the same. She had an edge about her. She seemed bitter and unhappy. She hardly laughed or smiled, and she didn't cry anymore when she heard Beethoven.

Questions for Group Discussion

1. Why did Ellen end up so miserable?
2. What are some indications that Ellen is a perfectionist?
3. If Ellen were to come to you for advice, what would you tell her?
4. What would it take to restore Ellen's love for music?
5. What kind of frustration is in store for those who know or live with a perfectionist?
6. What do you think God feels for the perfectionist?
7. Have you ever walked away from a conversation kicking yourself for something you said? Have you done this recently?
8. Have you ever made a mistake in a performance and played it over and over in your mind? What was that like for you?

Signs of Perfectionism

Like all the scenarios in this book, Ellen's story is based on someone I encountered during my ministry. But watching Ellen struggle with perfectionism hit me in a deeply personal way. Her suffering grieved me, moved me, and scared me all at the same time, because I could see that I was heading in the same direction. My perfectionistic tendencies were hindering me from truly enjoying music and were threatening to rob me of the joy of being an artist. Like Ellen, I was starting to dread music because it constantly reminded me of how much I didn't measure up. I could see that I was heading for a crisis if I didn't deal with my perfectionism.

My readers might notice that this topic of perfectionism comes up in every one of my books, for this has been a lifelong battle for me. The learnings I share come out of my journey. I realize, however, that I am not alone. Hundreds of artists have shared with me their struggles and frustrations with perfectionism. I know some who gave up their art because they didn't know how to deal with this drive that many of us have to be perfect.

Now, some may be wondering, *What's wrong with wanting things to be perfect? Isn't that only going to make my art better?* I get that question often when I speak on college campuses, usually from students training to be virtuoso musicians. The problem is that perfectionism is rarely confined to just our artistic endeavors but typically carries over into other areas of our lives, putting demands on us that we can't live up to and making us more demanding of others. As we shall see, striving for perfection does not necessarily make you a better artist, and it certainly doesn't make you a better person. Let's begin our discussion by probing some of the telltale signs of perfectionism.

MAXIMIZING THE NEGATIVE, MINIMIZING THE POSITIVE

The perfectionist tends to maximize the negative and minimize the positive. I do this a lot. I can get ten letters of encouragement and one from somebody who's unhappy with my work; guess which letter gets all my attention? The negative one. I'll fret about that one negative comment, playing it over and over in my mind. Forget that ten people took the time to write me and affirm my efforts. I dwell on that one negative response to my work. We shouldn't ignore negative feedback, but to blow it out of proportion isn't right either.

Obsessing with the negative aspects of a service or a performance creates what some refer to as the "dot syndrome," where you make one little mistake and you keep replaying it in your mind. It's a loss of perspective. Instead of looking at the big picture, we're obsessed with one tiny dot. It's like the artist who's just finished a magnificent painting and notices one microscopic blemish, so he throws out the entire painting. For a perfectionist caught in the downward spiral of the dot syndrome, one thing gone wrong means everything's gone wrong.

Several years ago, I wrote an arrangement of an old hymn for a Thanksgiving service at my church. I treated it in a variety of styles, and it was supposed to be fun, celebratory, and worshipful. In those days, we didn't play to a click track. It was my job as the bandleader to set tempos and keep everyone together. Unfortunately, I counted off one section of this arrangement at a tempo that was too slow. I couldn't get the band back on track, so the arrangement played on at the wrong speed. It was quite the train wreck. The rest of the service went very well, but I went home depressed because of that one short section of a song ironically titled "Count Your Blessings." I was convinced that the entire service was ruined and that I had spoiled worship for thousands of people.

Some of us make a mistake and we're utterly destroyed. We can't stand the thought that we messed up or that we let someone down. We beat ourselves up over things we regret saying or things we wish we had said. We can't seem to forgive ourselves for making the simplest of mistakes.

POLARIZED THINKING

Perfectionists can exhibit a type of polarized thinking that measures themselves and their work in extremes—either they're bona fide artists or they should give up even trying. A performance or service was either all good or all bad. Everything is black or white, night or day; there's no in-between.

This polarized thinking causes perfectionists to be

self-critical. They come down hard on themselves when they fail. They engage in a lot of negative self-talk. "I can't sing. I shouldn't even be on the worship team." In his book *Abba's Child*, Brennan Manning says, "It used to be that I never felt safe with myself unless I was performing flawlessly. My desire to be perfect had transcended my desire for God. Tyrannized by an all-or-nothing mentality, I interpreted weakness as mediocrity and inconsistency as a loss of nerve. I dismissed compassion and self-acceptance as inappropriate responses. My jaded perception of personal failure and inadequacy led to a loss of self-esteem, triggering episodes of mild depression and heavy anxiety. Unwittingly I had projected onto God my feelings about myself. I felt safe with him only when I saw myself as noble, generous, and loving, without scars, fears, or tears. Perfect!"[29] It's easy to see how artists with self-condemning thoughts bouncing around in their brains would develop a paralyzing fear of failure. If any of you are still thinking that perfectionism is okay, allow me to point out that you can't do your best work as an artist if you're constantly afraid to fail. Perfectionism stifles creativity and inhibits performance.

SELF-ESTEEM BASED ON WHAT YOU DO INSTEAD OF WHO YOU ARE

Because perfectionists can be highly self-critical, they often struggle with self-esteem. Manning notes that "one of the most shocking contradictions in the American church is the intense dislike many disciples of Jesus have for themselves. They are more displeased with their own shortcomings than they would ever dream of being with someone else's. They are sick of their own mediocrity and disgusted by their own inconsistency."[30] My dear artistic friend, when it reaches the point where your talent makes you feel worthless as a person, your self-esteem is too wrapped up in what you do instead of who you are.

HIGH AND UNREALISTIC EXPECTATIONS

The perfectionist often sets high, unrealistic expectations. I deal with this frequently, especially when it comes to a song I've written. The more effort I put into a song, the higher my expectations are for it to come off perfectly. Good is not good enough. So I walk into rehearsal or a service expecting perfection and I'm disappointed. I may even harbor resentment toward one of my musicians or tech people because I don't think they took the song as seriously as they should have. If you and I set unrealistic expectations, we're setting ourselves up for frustration and disappointment.

Setting unrealistic expectations can spill into other areas of our lives as well, causing discontent with our careers, our ministries, our marriages. That's why perfectionists live with a lot of "if only's." If only they had gone to that college, studied with that teacher, or made that audition. If only they were serving at that church instead of this church, or they married that person instead of this person. We somehow feel that our lives would be so much better if only we had been set up better to succeed.

I wonder whether we should spell perfection with the letter *i* in the middle instead of an *e*, because perfection really is "perfiction." It's pure fantasy to envision ourselves as being perfect. God is the only one who's perfect. Perfectionism is a subtle form of the sin Adam and Eve committed in the garden of Eden—wanting to be like God. Setting unrealistic expectations for ourselves and others to satisfy our perfectionism is unfair to all involved.

LOSS OF JOY

Continually striving for perfection can be exhausting and demoralizing, which explains why perfectionistic artists eventually lose their joy and burn out. Do you know any artists who, like Ellen in our opening scenario, gave up writing or performing because they couldn't live up to their standards? They feel under pressure all the time. And they wonder why writing or performing isn't fun anymore. Music is not enjoyable if it constantly reminds you that you don't measure up. Don't let perfectionism rob you of the joy of being an artist. Don't let it deprive you of the fulfillment and satisfaction that comes from using your God-given talent to glorify him.

Suggestions from a Die-Hard Perfectionist

As I've already shared, perfectionism is my biggest personal battle. So the following suggestions are based on what I've learned from dealing with this issue.

SAVOR THE POSITIVE

First, savor the positive. Because we tend to maximize the negative, we perfectionists need to celebrate anything and everything positive that comes our way. This means that we don't ignore the ten letters of encouragement that came with the negative one. We might even save those positive notes so we can read them again. It also means that we stop discounting compliments from people. Instead of writing off what they're saying, we make an effort to receive their encouraging words.

Some may be uncomfortable with the idea of savoring, because it sounds self-aggrandizing. Savoring, however, is not patting yourself on the back for a job well done. It's letting God pat you on the back for doing what he's called and equipped you to do. In that way, savoring becomes a worship experience in which you thank God for using you and your talent, for apart from him we can do nothing (John 15:5). If a service or an event goes well and you contributed to its success, it's okay to feel good about that and to celebrate what God did through your humble efforts.

After defeating the Philistines, King David returned the ark of the covenant to Jerusalem. The whole nation celebrated, and David was so overjoyed that he danced "with all his might" (2 Sam. 6:14). And why not? He was savoring a great work of God that he had the privilege to be a part of. David danced before the Lord with humility and joy. He wasn't taking the glory for himself. He was worshiping God. Maximizing the negative is self-centered because it focuses on us and our shortcomings. But savoring is God-centered because it celebrates God's gifting us and using us. Instead of downplaying the good things that happen when God uses you, try savoring, for God's glory, the good things God does through you.

My wife once told me something interesting about Amish crafts. The Amish purposely put a flaw somewhere in their handiwork. It could be a piece of thread that's out of line or a part of a quilt that's slightly off-center, but it's there to remind them that only God is perfect. The first time I taught my team at church about perfectionism, I wanted to give everyone a visual reminder to savor the good things God does in us and through us. My hardworking assistant at the time, Lisa Stone, graciously volunteered to cross-stitch the phrase "Savor it" for everyone on the team and put each finished piece in a nice frame. But in keeping with the Amish tradition that reminds us of our human frailty, Lisa put a slight mistake in each cross-stitch. She purposely didn't dot the *i* in the word *it* to remind us that only God is perfect.

BE KIND TO THE ARTIST IN YOU

Whether we perform or create, there's an artist inside who wants so much to blossom and flourish, to be able to grow, and to be given a chance to express. The way we treat each other goes a long way in whether that becomes possible, but the way we treat ourselves is equally important. Some of us are in situations in which it's difficult for the artist to flourish—a discouraging situation at church or too little encouragement or support at home. Some of us have fallen into patterns we learned in childhood, in which we put ourselves down when we feel we don't measure up. Ephesians 4:32 tells us to "be kind and compassionate to one another, forgiving each other, just as in Christ God forgave you." That's a great verse. Have you ever thought of applying it to yourself and the artist in you? As we've seen, perfectionists are overly critical of themselves and engage in a lot of negative self-talk. When we mistreat the artist in us, we diminish someone God created and loves. Some of us wouldn't dream of treating others as badly as we treat that artist inside us.

Please understand that I'm not against having high standards. But there is a fine line between having high standards and being obsessed with perfection. You can tell whether you're healthy in this area by how you respond to your own mistakes and the mistakes of others. A fellow artist who struggles with perfectionism once shared with me a new insight she was learning. "I don't mess up on purpose," she said, "so I just need to relax and not get so down on myself all the time." Easier said than done, of course, but I appreciate her efforts to be more gracious toward herself when she makes mistakes. Life as an artist is tough already. We don't need to make it worse by being our own worst enemy. The next time you're tempted to cut yourself down for not measuring up, remember that no one whom Christ died for deserves to be treated badly, not even you.

LOOK TO GOD FOR YOUR SELF-ESTEEM

Accolades and applause are nice, but you cannot build a healthy self-esteem on the approval of others. If you base your self-image on what you do instead of who you are, your self-respect will go up and down depending on your latest reviews. The key to a healthy self-image is not about doing. It's about being: being a beloved child of God. To arrive at a healthy view of yourself, build your self-esteem on who you are as God's beloved son or daughter.

I have struggled in the past with the concept of God's love. I know God loves the world, but does he love me? I know in my head that God loves me, but does he like me? How can what I know to be true on an intellectual level become a reality—something I feel and know to be true—in my heart?

The Bible teaches that God knows us intimately and loves us personally. The Psalms indicate that God delights in us (Pss. 18:19; 37:23; 41:11). Do you realize that God delights in you? He created you. He enjoys being with you and watching you become the person—the artist—he created you to be. He takes pleasure every time you use your talent—the talent he gave you—to glorify him.

Another passage that puts us in touch with God's love is Romans 8:38–39: "I am convinced that neither death nor life, neither angels nor demons, neither the present nor the future, nor any powers, neither height nor depth, nor anything else in all creation, will be able to separate us from the love of God that is in Christ Jesus our Lord." This verse has become especially meaningful to me because it reminds me that nothing—absolutely nothing—can separate me from the love of God. Even if I'm having trouble feeling his love, it's still there and nothing can take it away. If you struggle with feeling loved by God, I suggest memorizing verses like the ones I've just mentioned, so these truths can become etched deeply into your heart and soul. But I should warn you that it's not enough to memorize verses about God's love. At some point you've got to let him love you.

LET THE LORD LOVE YOU

Have you ever been sitting in church during worship and been overwhelmed by the thought that God loves you? What was your response? Have you ever sensed God trying to tell you that he is pleased with you or that he delights in you?

Did you ignore him when that happened? I've had experiences like that, and too often I've dismissed them, thinking that I'm making something up in my head, merely believing what I want to believe. But Scripture describes an angel appearing to Daniel to tell him that God loves him (Dan. 9:23; 10:11, 19). The original Hebrew is more explicit, indicating that Daniel is precious in the eyes of God, that God treasures him, and that he is God's beloved.[31] This idea that God goes out of his way to tell us personally that he loves us is rooted in Scripture.

One time I was working out at our neighborhood gym, and out of the blue I sensed God saying to me, "I am pleased with you." I hope that doesn't sound weird. I didn't hear a voice or anything. That thought just quietly but strongly entered my mind. At first I thought, *No, that's not from God. He's not trying to tell me that he's pleased with me. I must be making it up.* But then I realized I couldn't be making it up, because at the time I had been struggling severely with feelings of self-doubt and inadequacy. The thought occurred to me that perhaps God was trying to tell me he loves me. So I listened (as I continued my workout), and I sensed God saying to me, "And I like your music." Well, that began to move me to tears because I had been struggling with disappointment over my songwriting. *Lord, are you sure you like my music?* I asked. *You know I've written some real duds lately.* "I don't care," I sensed God saying. "I like them because you wrote them, and you're my beloved child." I had to leave the gym right then and there because I couldn't control my emotions. And it's not very manly to be lifting weights with tears streaming down your face. I bolted for the parking lot, sat in my car, and cried. I had an encounter with the love of God that was deep and real and personal. I shudder to think that I almost missed it. I almost dismissed it and ignored it.

We need to listen to God's truth about who we are in him; but somewhere along the way we have to let it touch us deeply. First John 4:16 says, "We have come to know and have believed the love which God has for us" (NASB). You and I will never come to know and believe that God loves us if we refuse to receive his love. You have to let God love you.[32]

SET REALISTIC EXPECTATIONS

Does God expect us to perform perfectly? Of course not. Can God use someone or something that is imperfect? Can he use a song that is sung or played imperfectly? Of course he can; he does it all the time. The major source of frustration in my life stems from my walking into situations with expectations that are unreasonably high. The psalmist suggests that we base our expectations not on what we want but on what God wants. "My soul, wait thou only upon God," he writes, "for my expectation is from him" (Ps. 62:5 KJV). God is in the business of saving souls. So what's more important: that our efforts come off perfectly or that God's name be praised and that lost people come to know him? Try to keep things in perspective.

REDISCOVER THE JOY OF BEING AN ARTIST

Perfectionism has robbed too many artists of the joy of using their talents for the Lord. Winston Churchill is best known as a statesman, speaker, author, and soldier, but he was also an avid painter. He once told a fellow artist, "Now don't go out and imagine you are going to paint a masterpiece, because you won't. Go out and paint for the fun and enjoyment of it."[33] Good advice for artists in the church! Have fun and enjoy using your talents for the Lord. Jacqueline du Pré was a virtuoso cellist who died in 1987 at the age of forty-two from multiple sclerosis. Every picture I've ever seen of Jacqueline shows her playing the cello with an infectious smile on her face. She obviously enjoyed making music. I invite you to rediscover the joy of being an artist. Revel in the pleasure of doing what God's gifted you to do.

Pursuing Excellence

Those with formal training in the arts often have a difficult time accepting the idea that perfectionism is a negative. Many of us were taught that the great artists, master composers, and virtuoso performers were relentless perfectionists. I argue that it was not their perfectionism that made them great, it was their pursuit of excellence. My longtime friend Nancy Beach defines excellence as "doing the best you can with what you have." No matter how much or how little talent we've been given, we can all try to do our best. Note the word try. God understands that we're not perfect. All he's asking of us is to try to do our best. You're not expected to do somebody else's best; you're expected to perform or create consistently at your level of ability. This means that you don't have to be a professional to do the best you can with what you have. You don't even have to be an accomplished artist. You just have to be willing to try to do your best.

Pursuing excellence glorifies God. We are made in the image of a prolifically creative God. His handiwork, the entire created order, is adorned with breathtaking beauty and awe-inspiring majesty. Seven times during the Genesis account of creation, God observes what he's created and says, "It is good." We serve a God who delights in creativity and values doing things with excellence. We honor him when we try to do the best we can with the talents he's given us. I believe that pursuing excellence is a healthy alternative to perfectionism. Let's examine further what it means to pursue excellence.

Artistic Integrity—Developing Skill

Excellence in the arts calls for artistic integrity, which simply means that an artist performs or creates with skill. Psalm

33:3 tells us to "play skillfully." The psalmist doesn't say anything about playing perfectly. Instead of striving for perfection, try to do what you do as skillfully as you can. Do your best with the talent God gave you. There was a vocalist in the Old Testament named Kenaniah who had a reputation for being skillful (1 Chron. 15:22). He was singled out for leadership and responsibility because of his talent. He had artistic integrity. Like Kenaniah, we too need to shoot high artistically. Franky Schaeffer believes that Christians, of all people, "should be addicted to quality and integrity in every area, not be looking for excuses for second-best. We must resist this onslaught. We must demand higher standards. We must look for people with real creative integrity and talent, or we must not dabble in these creative fields at all. All of this does not mean that there is no room for the first halting steps, for experimentation, for mistakes and for development. But it does mean that there is no room for lazy, entrenched, year after year established mediocrity, unchanging and unvaried."[34]

To maintain artistic integrity, we need to take seriously the development of our skills. First Chronicles 25:7 tells us that the artists in the Old Testament were all trained. We too need training and ongoing development. We should be open to taking classes and lessons or getting good coaching. We need to read books and magazines that will help us improve our craft. How can you develop as a musician, writer, filmmaker, audio engineer, lighting director, actor, dancer, or painter without ongoing training? What can you do to challenge yourself artistically?

We can learn a great deal by exposing ourselves to great art. Don't stay away from great art just because it's not "Christian." Schaeffer points out that there are only two kinds of art—good art and bad art. "There is good secular art and bad secular art. There is good art made by Christians and bad art made by Christians (and all the shadings in between)."[35] We can learn a great deal and improve our skills by exposing ourselves to quality art inside and outside the church. Philippians 4:8 instructs us to let our minds dwell on things that display excellence. We should be attending art exhibits, concerts, plays, movies, and musicals to broaden our artistic horizons. That's part of our ongoing development as artists. The idea here is to expose yourself to excellence, which unfortunately would exclude much of what's offered by mainstream media. Don't subject yourself to brain-numbing entertainment when you could be reading a good book, listening to a masterful recording, taking in a first-rate play, or visiting an art gallery.

Artistic integrity involves hard work. There is a price to be paid for excellence. Don't kid yourself and think otherwise. If you want to pursue excellence in the arts, you need to put forth effort. This is no time for us artists in the church to be lazy. Being lazy with our talent is more a sign of being comfortable than of being committed. I recall a T-shirt that read, "Success comes before work only in the dictionary." Wise words for artists to heed. Remember, God has entrusted each of us with a talent, and we are accountable for how we steward that gift (Matt. 25:14–30 NASB). Working at our craft is how we steward our talents. I like what the famous conductor Sir Georg Solti said, near the end of his life, about the need for artists to work hard. He said, "I feel more strongly than ever that I have an endless amount of studying and thinking to do in order to become the musician I would like to be."[36] Those words were spoken by a man who was already an international success and in his mideighties.

Giving God Our Best

One time our guitar player was having a hard time getting one of his strings in tune. After several attempts, he finally threw up his hands and said, "It's good enough for church work." That remark, along with the attitude that comes with it, is one of my pet peeves. This mindset has no place in the heart of an artist. Some of us in the church do only enough to get by. God deserves so much more than that. He deserves our best effort.

In the Old Testament, God tells David to build an altar, and a man named Araunah offers to give David everything he needs to build it. But David refuses, saying he didn't want to offer the Lord what cost him nothing (2 Sam. 24:24). David didn't want to do anything halfheartedly for God. In the same way, we need to avoid a lackadaisical attitude in serving the Lord.

The artists who worked on the temple used the best gold and the best clay they could find, because they wanted to give God their best (2 Chron. 3:6; 4:17). In Malachi 1, God reproves the nation of Israel because they weren't bringing their best sacrifices to the altar. They were offering blemished animals that were sick, old, or lame. It doesn't honor God when we bring him less than our best. Colossians 3:23 says, "Whatever you do, work at it with all your heart, as working for the Lord, not for human masters." My fellow artists, God is worthy of our best efforts. Let's honor him by giving him our best.

Because I'm addressing artists who might struggle with perfectionism, I need to clarify that the notion of giving God our best should never be used as an excuse to become obsessed with perfection. Again, pursuing excellence means doing the best we can with what we have. And you will not do that perfectly. Bringing God our best does not demand perfect effort.

Effective Communication

Pursuing excellence also entails learning how to communicate effectively through your art. At its best, art conveys a message, an idea, a mood, a feeling. Every art form therefore requires a certain degree of skill in communicating meaning and emotion. Interestingly, Paul cites examples from the world of music to underscore the importance of clarity in speaking. "Even in the case of lifeless things that make sounds, such as the pipe or harp, how will anyone know what tune is being played unless there is a distinction in the notes? Again, if the trumpet does not sound a clear call, who will get ready for battle? So it is with you. Unless you speak intelligible words with your tongue, how will anyone know what you are saying?" (1 Cor. 14:7–9). If we artists give no thought as to how to communicate a piece, its message will lack clarity and power. I've been moved by singers whose technique was raw but whose communication skills were strong. An artist who has great technique but doesn't know how to communicate clearly and effectively moves no one. Christian art will never become a force to be reckoned with if we ignore what it takes to communicate with passion and meaning.

In my experience, it's church vocalists who are most oblivious to the need for good communication skills. There's been a sentiment in the church for too long that singers who perform without any facial expression or emotion are somehow less distracting and more spiritual. The stereotypical church vocalist sings with arms perfectly still, no passion, looking straight down at the music. No eye contact, no meaningful gestures. The irony here rests in just how unnatural that is. When we're talking about something important to us, we don't stand at attention like robots. We move our arms to emphasize a point. Our faces register emotion that matches our words. We look at people when we talk to them. Vocalists, do you think about how to communicate what you're singing, or do you just learn notes? Does your face reflect what the lyrics are saying? Are you using gestures that are meaningful and natural for you?

Some of us are stiff and reserved on the platform because we're overly concerned with how we look. We're too self-conscious. Speechwriter Peggy Noonan offers helpful advice on getting over ourselves. "When you forget yourself and your fear, when you get beyond self-consciousness because your mind is thinking about what you are trying to communicate, you become a better communicator."[37] Professional dancer and choreographer Mark Morris also suggests throwing ourselves into what we're doing to avoid focusing on ourselves. "As a performer there's nothing better than moments where you feel that you have the option—within the given text—to do exactly as you want, where you're not worried about what you look like or whether you've warmed up enough. You just seem to be involved in a pure expression which is completely appropriate."[38]

We artists in the church need to take communication seriously because we've been entrusted to communicate the good news of Jesus Christ. We have the most important message there is, so let's communicate it boldly, passionately, and clearly.

Spiritual Preparation

Last, pursuing excellence necessitates spiritual preparation. I've discovered over the years how crucial it is for Christian artists to prepare their hearts and minds spiritually before they create or perform. The apostle Paul knew the importance of spiritual preparation before ministry. After his dramatic conversion, he didn't hit the lecture circuit right away. He spent several years in relative obscurity, training for ministry. He already had speaking and teaching gifts, but he needed to prepare himself spiritually for the mission to which God called him (Gal. 1:15–2:1). And this was one of the greatest religious scholars of his day. Like Paul, we too need to make spiritual preparation a priority every time we lead God's people in worship.

Most of what I've learned about spiritual preparation I've gleaned from the gifted singers I've worked with over the years. I've seen some of them take lyrics to a song they're working on and journal on every line of the piece. Others did Bible studies on the main theme of a song or meditated on related Scriptures. I've heard singers share insights they've gained from applying the truth of a particular song to their own lives. When it comes to ministering in the church, spiritual preparation is every bit as important as musical practice and rehearsal.

Come to Me

I'd like us to imagine what Jesus might say to the perfectionist. I believe the Son of God would look us straight in the eyes, hold out his hand, and say, "Come to me, all you who are weary and burdened, and I will give you rest. Take my yoke upon you and learn from me, for I am gentle and humble in heart, and you will find rest for your souls. For my yoke is easy and my burden is light" (Matt. 11:28–30). That's a great passage for artists who are weighed down with perfectionism, who have become weary trying to live up to their own expectations, who are heavy-laden with negative self-talk. Jesus says, "Come to me just as you are, warts and all. Come to me and be free from the pressure of your self-inflicted perfectionism." Notice that Jesus is not the slave-driving, impossible-to-please God that we make him out to be. He is gentle and humble.

Sounds inviting, doesn't it? Compared with the demands we perfectionists put on ourselves, his yoke is easy and his load is light. Besides, he's there, ready and willing to help shoulder our burdens. My fellow artists, find rest and relief from the bondage of your perfectionism in Jesus.

Follow-Up Questions for Group Discussion

1. Do you see any signs of perfectionism in your life? Go through the following list and put a check by any of the tendencies you see in yourself.
   - ____Minimizing the positive, maximizing the negative
   - ____The dot syndrome (looking at a small flaw and ignoring the overall good)
   - ____Polarized thinking (either all bad or all good)
   - ____Negative self-talk
   - ____Self-esteem based on what you do instead of who you are in Christ
   - ____Unrealistically high expectations
   - ____Loss of joy

2. How can you savor something you've done recently that God has blessed?

3. What's preventing you from knowing and believing that God loves you?

4. In what situations do you tend to set expectations that are too high? What suggestions do you have to help someone rediscover the joy of being an artist?

5. How would you express in your own words the difference between striving for perfection and pursuing excellence?

6. What is the next step for you in your development as an artist? What can you do to challenge yourself artistically?
7. What does it mean for you to bring God your best in your role at church?
8. How can you improve your communication skills as an artist?
9. What can you do to prepare yourself spiritually for the next time you serve?

PERSONAL ACTION STEPS

1. Share your struggles with perfectionism with a trusted friend and ask him or her to pray for you.
2. Schedule an artistic outing, such as a concert or play.
3. Find the verse in the Bible that speaks most convincingly to you about God's love for you personally. Meditate on that verse and memorize it.
4. Identify steps you can take to further develop your artistic or communication skills. Run those ideas by your ministry leader to get his or her input.
5. Spend time praying and reading God's Word for the purpose of preparing yourself spiritually to minister to your congregation this weekend.

CHAPTER 5

HANDLING CRITICISM

JUSTIN IS THE TECHNICAL DIRECTOR AT Southport Community Church. In addition to mixing audio, he also runs lights and video. He puts in a lot of hours volunteering at the church. For most every service or event, he's the first one there and the last one to leave. He enjoys what he does at church, but lately he's been at odds with Sam, the new worship leader. Sam's got all sorts of new ideas that put Justin on tilt every time they talk.

When they first met, Sam gave Justin a long list of changes he wanted to make. First, he wanted to lengthen rehearsal time, which meant that Justin would have to be at the church even earlier. Justin was already stressed out from all the hours he was putting in. Sam wanted new video screens, he wanted to move the speakers in the sanctuary, and he wanted to mic the drums differently. Justin didn't see the need for any of those changes.

Particularly challenging has been the new evaluation meeting that Justin has to attend every Monday morning. The key leaders involved in putting the service together meet with Sam and the pastor at a restaurant to critique the previous day's service. The meeting is hard for Justin. Every time anything negative comes up about the sound or the lighting, he gets defensive. One time the pastor asked why his lapel mic sounded as if it was on the verge of feedback during the sermon, and Justin snapped back, saying, "Well, if I had some decent equipment to work with, we wouldn't have this problem." No one knew what to say. The conversation moved on, but Justin wasn't really listening during the rest of the meeting. He was lost in a series of negative and defensive thoughts. *They have no idea how hard I work. . . . I'm doing the best I can. . . . They're lucky to have me. . . . No one else would put up with all this aggravation. . . . I don't get paid to do this.*

Sam has made several suggestions about the overall mix that haven't set well with Justin. During one rehearsal Sam asked for less reverb on the group vocals and more warmth. This made Justin angry. "I know what I'm doing!" he wanted to shout. In spite of being offended, Justin complied with the request, and even he had to admit that less reverb gave the sound more clarity. To add insult to injury, several people complimented Justin on the mix as they left church that morning. They said they could hear the lyrics better. Justin appreciated their encouragement, but he still didn't like the idea of this new guy Sam telling him how to do his job.

The communication between the two men is like a tug-of-war. Every time Sam makes a suggestion, Justin asks why and then grudgingly complies. As a result, there is tension at every sound check, every meeting, and every service. People feel as if they have to walk on eggshells when they're around Justin, because he takes even the slightest bit of criticism so personally. He seems to have a short fuse.

The straw that broke the camel's back was an incident that occurred last week. During the sound check, two microphones that had been working erratically went dead. Sam had asked Justin to get new ones and had authorized the purchase two weeks prior. Justin had been meaning to buy the new mics but hadn't gotten around to it. He dropped the ball. When Sam questioned him about it, Justin became defensive and angry. "If you want new mics, get 'em yourself!" he yelled.

During the service Justin could hardly concentrate. He was seething. His thoughts outpaced his emotions. *What right does this newcomer have to make such outrageous demands all the time? If it wasn't for me, this service wouldn't even be happening. I deserve to be treated better than this.* The anger burned hotter and hotter until Justin couldn't take it anymore. In the middle of the opening song, he turned the board off, there was a loud boom, the music stopped, and the sanctuary fell silent.

Congregation members turned and watched Justin storm out of the sound booth. He continued through the lobby and out the front door of the church. After the service, Sam tried several times to call Justin, but Justin never picked up.

Questions for Group Discussion

1. Why, do you think, did Justin react negatively to every suggestion Sam made?
2. Why did Justin take criticism so personally?
3. What would you suggest Justin do to mend his relationship with Sam?
4. What should Sam do next to try to patch things up with Justin?
5. Is there any way the tension between Justin and Sam could have been avoided? What could they have done differently that would have enabled them to work together more harmoniously?
6. How does a defensive spirit affect rehearsals?
7. How do you think an artist should handle criticism?
8. What happens to an artist when he or she is not open to constructive criticism?
9. What is the best way to give feedback to an artist?

Three Dangers of Defensiveness

Those of us with artistic temperaments get defensive sometimes when we're criticized. When we're overly sensitive, a minor criticism can get blown out of proportion. At times we're offended even when no offense was intended; we take things too personally. We may have a defensive spirit because of pride, fear, insecurity, or a dysfunctional upbringing, but whatever the reason, it can stifle us relationally and spiritually. And it can have devastating effects on our ministry and on the team with which we serve. Very often the person who's overly defensive doesn't realize it. You may think this is not a problem for you, but believe me, if you're a sensitive artist, the potential is always there for you to take something more personally than you should. Artists can also be stubborn; we want to do things our way, and when anybody challenges that, we get angry.

Scenarios like Justin and Sam's are all too common, especially among artists. I've seen instrumentalists get defensive about intonation. I had a flute player tell me that she never plays out of tune, because her instrument was pitched at 440 at the factory. I had to break the news to her that perhaps the problem was not her instrument. I've watched singers get defensive when they're having difficulty learning a part. I've also seen songwriters respond to well-meaning suggestions with indignation. "How dare you criticize what I wrote.

This came from God; I'm not changing a thing. It's fine just the way it is!" A defensive spirit isn't healthy for you or your team, and it does nothing to advance your artistry. The Bible insists that it's foolish to despise feedback (Prov. 1:7). Let's examine three reasons why.

1. DEFENSIVENESS ALIENATES US FROM OTHERS

Being defensive cuts you off from meaningful relationships. People who are quick to defend themselves are not very approachable. When people feel they have to be extra sensitive around a certain individual, they avoid that person because interacting with them is so draining. Sometimes we get defensive to avoid getting hurt or being rejected. Yet the very thing we're trying to avoid inevitably happens, because people tend to stay away from overly sensitive individuals. Chronic defensiveness leaves a person feeling lonely, bitter, and resentful.

2. DEFENSIVENESS KEEPS US FROM THE TRUTH

Being defensive prevents us from knowing the truth about ourselves and our abilities. People tend to withhold their honest thoughts and opinions from overly sensitive people for fear of hurting them. Too often I've stretched the truth with a defensive artist to make that person feel better, or held something back so as not to upset them. Afterward I'd kick myself because I let the person's hypersensitivity keep me from saying something they needed to hear. Being deceived about your abilities is far worse than knowing and accepting your strengths and weaknesses. Artists who face their shortcomings are able to deal with them and grow. Even though it can be hard to hear, the truth is always more helpful than a lie.

3. DEFENSIVENESS KEEPS US FROM BEING ALL WE CAN BE

Being defensive keeps us from achieving our full potential as artists. I've dealt with songwriters who requested my honest feedback on their latest song, only to get offended when I pointed out a few problems. They obviously didn't want my honest opinion. It's made me wary of critiquing original songs. When we allow ourselves to be defensive, we stop growing as people and as artists. Listening to criticism and responding to suggestions is one of the ways artists through the ages have improved their craft. Defensiveness cuts us off from what can help us flourish as artists: constructive feedback. There is much we can learn from negative critique.

Taking Offense

Because many artists are sensitive people, we pick up vibes from others. We walk into a room and can sense a mood. Or we notice someone and have a hunch as to what they're feeling. But we mustn't assume that our intuition is always correct. We need to be careful that we don't pick up on something that's not there. More to the point, we need to make sure we don't become quickly offended. Scripture warns us not to take offense where none was intended (Prov. 3:30). Ecclesiastes cautions against taking what people say too personally (7:21). We are not to be easily provoked (1 Cor. 13:4–5). Proverbs 11:27 says, "Whoever seeks good finds favor, but evil comes to one who searches for it." So be careful not to take someone's negative comment and blow it out of proportion; don't make it bigger than it is.

When the elders of Israel approached Samuel and asked him to appoint a king over them, he was offended. He took it as an indictment against his leadership. He took it as a slap in the face because he was old and his sons were doing a poor job of leading the nation. The Lord told Samuel, "Listen to all that the people are saying to you; it is not you they have rejected, but they have rejected me as their king" (1 Sam. 8:7). In a sense God was saying, "Don't make a mountain out of a molehill, Samuel. This isn't about you, so don't take it personally."

Like Samuel, we artists are often quickly offended; our egos bruise too easily. A single comment or someone's facial expression can convince us that the person is against us or trying to undermine us. But that's not always the case. The problem might be a small misunderstanding, or perhaps we're being overly sensitive. The nation of Israel went to the brink of civil war because of a simple misunderstanding (Joshua 22). In the end, cooler heads prevailed, and when the people sat down and talked, they realized it was much ado about nothing.

When in doubt, check it out. If you're taking offense because of something you heard secondhand, go to the person and ask about what was said. If you're taking something personally but are not sure it was meant that way, find out. Don't assume. I don't know how often I've been offended and have gone to the person only to find that I took what was said too personally, that I misunderstood what was said, or that I misinterpreted the person's motives. So be careful not to take offense when none was intended.

Personal Blind Spot

If it sounds like I know a thing or two about being defensive, it's because this was a major blind spot in my life until someone confronted me about it. I was in my early twenties when a coworker pulled me aside and said, "Brother, we all feel like we have to walk on eggshells around you. You get so defensive whenever anyone says anything remotely negative." I was shocked to realize that people were not only avoiding me but also withholding valuable feedback from me because I was a defensive person.

I spent the next week meeting with everyone on the team and apologizing for alienating them and not listening to their input. I promised that from that day on, I was going to be open to any and all criticism. I gave them the freedom to speak truth to me. And I invited them to call me on it if they saw any shred of defensiveness. I didn't want to go on being that guy who was stubbornly defensive.

I owe a debt of gratitude to that coworker who pulled me aside and pointed out my blind spot. He spoke the truth in love. Years later I entered into a relationship with a music publisher. My main contact at the company called me to give me her feedback on a song I had submitted. At the end of the conversation, she expressed appreciation for my being open to evaluation, adding that I would go far as a writer because of it. If she only knew how I used to be. I shudder to think where I would be today had my friend at work not mustered the courage to confront me about my defensiveness.

Responding to Feedback

Because of my own battle with this issue, I understand why artists get defensive. Our artistry can be such a personal expression of ourselves. We invest extraordinary amounts of time and energy into what we do. We put our stamp on it, so an artist pours both heart and soul into his or her work. When someone attacks our work, it feels like they're attacking us.

As a songwriter, I'm well aware of the intensity surrounding the creative process. When I'm writing a song, I can't think about anything else. I become obsessed with this tune that plays incessantly in my brain; it keeps me up all night. I agonize over every word of the lyrics. I'm excited and can't wait to play it for someone. But when I do, I feel extremely vulnerable. My biggest fear is that my listeners will kill my little brainchild before it has a chance to succeed. I understand how difficult it can be to separate ourselves from our work and look at it objectively.

So how do you overcome defensiveness? How can you respond to feedback in a nondefensive manner? How can you remain sensitive without being overly sensitive?

GREET FEEDBACK AS YOUR FRIEND

First, look at all criticism as potentially constructive. David was an artist who realized the value of criticism. In Psalm 141:5 he said, "Let a righteous man strike me—that is a kindness; let him rebuke me—that is oil on my head. My head will not refuse it." God can use honest critique to bring growth into your life—spiritual growth as well as artistic growth. So greet feedback as your friend.

An obscure character in the Bible, named Apollos, exemplifies what it means to greet feedback as your friend (Acts 18:24–28). Apollos was apparently a gifted teacher and leader, but his theology was a little off-center. Two people,

Priscilla and Aquila (one of the great wife-and-husband teams in Scripture), pulled Apollos aside and confronted him about his theology. We don't know exactly what was said, but we do know that Apollos was faced with a choice. Either he was going to listen to truth and gain from it, or he was going to take offense and ignore the truth. It's obvious that Apollos was open to the truth and regarded feedback as beneficial, because after he listened to Priscilla and Aquila, his ministry flourished. "He was a great help to those who by grace had believed. For he vigorously refuted his Jewish opponents in public debate, proving from the Scriptures that Jesus was the Messiah" (vv. 27–28). Apollos went on to do great things for God because he was open to constructive criticism. Apollos's contribution to the church would have been lost forever had he not listened to wise advice from others. My fellow artists, be open to critique. As we've seen, it could prove to be in your best interest in the long run. Greet feedback as a friend, not an enemy. The real enemy is our defensiveness.

RESPOND WITH GRACE

Even if we're convinced that constructive criticism is good for us, it can still be difficult to know how to respond to suggestions or criticism with grace instead of anger. James 1:19 shows us how to do that: "Everyone should be quick to listen, slow to speak and slow to become angry."

Be quick to listen. Sometimes we're too busy being defensive to really listen. Negative feedback can trigger all sorts of negative self-talk. Our brains get hijacked in those moments and prevent us from listening to what's being said. Instead of being quick to justify yourself, listen first. Listen without being threatened. Remember, you are not someone who has to have your giftedness or worth validated every time something negative is hinted at. You are a beloved child of God. Listen to the opinions of others as someone who is secure in God's love. Receive what they say without blowing it up to be bigger than it is.

Be slow to speak. Don't be so quick to defend yourself. Proverbs 18:17 says, "The first to speak seems right, until someone comes forward and cross-examines." Be careful not to dismiss someone's negative critique too soon, because someone else could come along and corroborate their view. It would be sad to get to the end of our lives and realize that we had been deceived about ourselves simply because we refused to entertain the possibility that we were flawed.

Be slow to become angry. More often than not, when I respond impulsively out of anger, I say or do something I later regret. Try not to let anger take over. Take a step back. Cool down. Sometimes we get angry and defensive and take things in ways they were never intended to be taken. Being quick to listen and slow to speak can enable you to be slow to anger. You will also put yourself in a position to receive negative reviews with grace.

BE DISCERNING

When you open yourself to constructive criticism, you may get conflicting opinions that'll make your head spin. How do you know what's from God and what isn't? The writer of Proverbs asserts that simple people believe anything, "but the prudent give thought to their steps" (14:15). Handling criticism in a healthy way doesn't mean we regard every negative comment as true; it means we learn to discern the truth and let the rest fall by the wayside.

In Proverbs 15:31, we learn that the person who "heeds life-giving correction will be at home among the wise." Learning to deal with criticism in a constructive way can help us grow in wisdom to the point where we can discern what is from God. When encountering feedback, we need to ask ourselves, "Is any part of what I'm hearing true?" When you have trouble gaining clarity on that question, run your reactions by a trusted friend who's not afraid to be honest with you. Eventually you'll learn what feedback to take seriously and what you can ignore. You'll be secure enough to say to yourself, *Yeah, that's true. I could really grow in that area* or *I'm grateful for feedback, but I don't think that fits with what others have told me about my work.* Growing in discernment can help you gain greater objectivity regarding your negative press.

BE TEACHABLE

Welcoming feedback opens us up to the possibility that we might learn something that could make us better artists. We can swallow our pride and concede that no matter how accomplished we are, we can always improve. Not all feedback is given with sensitivity, but we can still learn from it. You're always going to run into the tactless individual who speaks without thinking. We need to learn to listen to what even those people are saying and overlook how they're saying it. Not all feedback is given with good intentions, but you can take what is helpful and leave the rest. Even if the criticism wasn't offered in love, you can turn it into something beneficial by asking yourself, "What can I learn from this criticism that can help me grow as an artist?" That's a sure way to make criticism work for you instead of against you.

I used to think that if someone pointed out a flaw in a song I wrote, it meant I wasn't a good songwriter. But I discovered that even the best writers solicit feedback; they're constantly reworking their material. They have a teachable spirit.

Remaining teachable allows us to learn from our mistakes. If your error was caused by a lack of preparation, be better prepared next time out. If you need to brush up on some technique or take a few lessons, do it. If you're having a mental block with lyrics, memorize those words until you're sick and tired of them. And then memorize them some more.

If you had some rough spots in rehearsal, work them out before the service. Learn all you can from your mistakes.

LEARN HOW TO FAIL GRACIOUSLY

It's okay to fail. No one succeeds every time. You and I will make mistakes, so we need to learn how to fail graciously. We need to own up to our mistakes, not run away from them or pass on responsibility to someone else. No one's expecting perfection (except maybe us), so we don't need to defend ourselves every time we fail. When we mess up, let's admit it, learn from it, and move on. Just because we fail doesn't mean we're failures. Giuseppe Verdi wrote fifteen operas that bombed before he wrote *Rigoletto* at the age of thirty-eight. From that point on, he was famous the world over as one of Italy's best opera composers. Verdi didn't give up or consider himself a failure just because he failed.

Forgive Those Who Have Hurt You

Have you ever been hurt by someone's harsh criticism? Were there any negative words spoken to you early in life that, now as an adult, you can't seem to shake? Some of us are habitually defensive because we've been wounded by some cruel or thoughtless comment from a parent or other authority figure in our past. Defensiveness becomes a means of protecting ourselves from ever being hurt like that again. I know artists who are in bondage to bitterness because they had a bad experience at an audition. The painful memory triggers the fear that they're not good enough.

The only way to be free from this vicious cycle is to forgive those who hurt you. Scripture says that no matter who it is, no matter what that person said, if we have anything against anyone, we need to forgive that person just as God has forgiven us (Col. 3:12–13). If it's hard to forgive someone who's wounded you with negative words, ask the Lord to help you want to forgive that person. Ask God to work in your life to get you to the point where you can truly forgive. Forgiving someone who spoke hurtful things to you can set you free from the bondage of those negative words and prevent them from holding you back as an artist. Forgiveness is a major step in the process of undoing the hurt. Let the power of forgiveness restore your heart and soul.

Defensiveness regarding Sin

If there is an area of habitual sin or willful disobedience in your life, I hope you will be open to the truth when confronted about it. Living in denial only makes it harder on yourself, because no one can help you if you don't think there's a problem or if you're lying about it. God is not pleased when we live in denial concerning sin. "You say, 'I am innocent; he is not angry with me.' But I will pass judgment on you because you say, 'I have not sinned'" (Jer. 2:35). Living in denial can be exhausting and draining. David tried to cover up his sin with Bathsheba, but when confronted by Nathan, Israel's king finally admitted his guilt, repented, and got right with God (2 Sam. 12:13). In Psalm 32, David describes from firsthand experience the agony of trying to live in denial about sin. "When I kept silent, my bones wasted away through my groaning all day long. For day and night your hand was heavy on me; my strength was sapped as in the heat of summer" (vv. 3–4).

I once spent two hours with a man who kept denying he had a serious problem with lust until he finally broke down and confessed to being involved with pornography and prostitution. It took us two hours to cut through the deception about his sin. Scripture encourages us to bring our wrongful behavior and our addictions to the light (Eph. 5:11). Trying to hide your sin is a waste of time, because your sin will inevitably find you out (Num. 32:23). Covering up sin takes more energy than confessing it.

Giving Feedback

My hope is that we will all become more open to receiving constructive criticism, but what about those giving the feedback? How can pastors, ministry leaders, friends, and spouses offer evaluation on an artist's work without demoralizing the artist? How can churches that evaluate services do it in a way that edifies? I've seen artists near tears because of criticism delivered without any sensitivity. My own confidence has been shaken at times by a poorly communicated critique. I've also known writers who lost their desire to write after being barraged with feedback that was given in a hurtful manner. No one really means for this to happen, and I think it's more a matter of ignorance than anything else.

What makes criticism constructive is the way it's delivered. If it's not offered in a loving way, it can do more harm than good. The truth must be spoken in love (Eph. 4:15). Constructive criticism must be truthful. Don't lie about the quality of someone's work. Be honest. Don't say something you don't mean. But speak the truth with love. Say it with tenderness and sensitivity. Say it in a way that builds up the artist. You can criticize one performance or one aspect of a person's work constructively without tearing the person down. Artists need to be able to trust that the people giving them feedback believe in them and have their best interest in mind. "A word fitly spoken is like apples of gold in settings of silver" (Prov. 25:11 NKJV). Feedback given and received in an environment of love and trust is valuable and God-honoring. I believe that every ministry should set ground rules for evaluating services and events. While every artistic community is different, I'd like to offer some guidelines for giving feedback.

GIVE YOUR OVERALL REACTION FIRST

Let's pretend I'm a gifted carpenter and I build a beautiful table and bring it to you for your opinion. Your immediate response is positive, but you don't say so. Instead you notice a small, faint blemish at the base of one of the table legs. Without hesitating, you draw attention to the defect. You might be thinking that this is the most delightful table you've ever seen and that the flaw is inconsequential. But because the first words out of your mouth are negative, I conclude that the flaw is so big that it ruins the entire table. When appraising an artist's work, remember that he or she hears the first words out of your mouth as your overall reaction. The flaw at the base of the table was not your general reaction; it wasn't even your first reaction. Your overall reaction was that you were very impressed with my work, but you never said that. If you hate someone's work, you'll need to figure out how to say so in a loving way. But if your overall reaction is positive, communicate that and then go on to the negative. The negative is easier for artists to receive if they know you generally like their work in the first place.

TRY TO SAY SOMETHING POSITIVE

When giving feedback, always start by saying something positive. Even if your overall reaction is negative, try to find something positive to say. Treat artists (and all people) with dignity and respect. I've conducted hundreds of musical auditions over the years. No matter how bad the audition went, I've always tried to tell the artist what I enjoyed about their audition before sharing what bothered me, listing their strengths before discussing their weaknesses. Don't jump into the negative without saying something positive.

ACKNOWLEDGE EFFORT AND HARD WORK

Express appreciation for any extra effort that was put forth. It's demoralizing to work especially hard and feel as if no one noticed. Most people have no idea how many hours an artist puts in practicing, rehearsing, or creating. If the finished product doesn't turn out as well as everyone would have liked, it feels as if all that hard work was in vain. That can be a discouraging experience. Even if something didn't work or fell apart completely, express appreciation for any extra preparation or rehearsal. No one means to fail. Be sure to honor the effort even if it falls short.

Nehemiah didn't take all the credit for rebuilding the wall in Jerusalem. In chapter 3 of his narration, he mentions by name seventy-five people who labored diligently throughout the project. He even recorded for posterity the role they played, describing exactly what they did. Wise leaders acknowledge effort and hard work.

AVOID HYPERBOLE

Avoid extreme statements. Whether they're positive or negative, they do more harm than good. "That's the best song we've ever done!" or "She's our best singer!" I feel sorry for anyone who has to follow something or someone who's been crowned the best ever. One time during worship the band was noticeably out of sync for about eight measures. Later that week someone from the congregation told me that our little journey into polyrhythms made him feel uncomfortable, that it was the worst experience he'd ever had at our church. As the person in charge, I felt terrible, because I was responsible for this. I suggest we all avoid hyperbole when expressing such opinions. Extreme statements usually draw extreme reactions.

AVOID NEGATIVE COMPARISONS

When we don't like something, it's tempting to emphasize this by comparing it to something unfashionable or mediocre. At the music school where I studied composition, it was common to call something you disliked "warmed-over Tchaikovsky." This drove home the point that someone's music was passé. We need to avoid making those kinds of negative comparisons, because they can be very hurtful to an artist.

One time someone compared a song I had arranged to a recording by the group Up with People, a preppy group of folk singers from the 1960s. For someone trying to be cutting edge, it was quite the put-down. Negative comparisons like that are used to make a point—usually humorously—but there's always a better way to get the point across.

Be Open to the Truth about Yourself

One of the responsibilities of leading a worship ministry is to make sure that all staff and volunteers are operating out of their strengths. If everyone serves in areas for which they are well suited, both they and the ministry will flourish. This also means that if I, as a leader, put somebody in a position they're not cut out for, I'm depriving that person of true fulfillment in a different role that lines up better with his or her giftedness.

In one instance, assessing the talents of my personnel put me in a sticky situation. I had just started on staff at a church and had been given a mandate to improve the quality of the service, especially the music. One of my immediate challenges was that I inherited a handful of musicians whose skills I could not honestly affirm. I conferred with my colleagues to make sure I wasn't missing something, but they agreed with me that these musicians were not at the level we needed them to be. Wanting to give these faithful volunteers every opportunity to succeed, I invited them to reaudition. Their auditions, though, confirmed my suspicion that they lacked the talents required for our ministry. I spoke with each of these dear servants personally. In each case, I began by thanking them for their years of service and for the important role they played in our church. But then I told them that, in my opinion, they didn't have the abilities we needed for the next leg of the race. Understandably, this was hard to hear, and there were lots of angry tears.

A few years later I received a note from one of the women I let go. She gave me permission to share it. "When you told me that I didn't have the ability I needed to sing at church, I hated you. I had been singing in church all my life, and no one had ever told me that I couldn't sing. Your words were some of the most difficult words I had ever heard, but they forced me to face the possibility that maybe I wasn't a singer after all. So for the first time in my life, I got down on my knees and asked the Lord to show me what he wanted me to do with my gifts and abilities. He led me back to school and into counseling. Today I opened my own counseling practice and I owe it all to you. Thank you!"

Not all sticky situations have happy endings, but this sister demonstrates the value of being open to the truth about our strengths and weaknesses. The truth, no matter how hard it is to hear, will always set us free (John 8:32).

What hinders you from being open to the truth about yourself? Is it pride? Pride nearly kept Naaman from being healed (2 Kings 5:1–14). He couldn't be helped until he was able to swallow his pride. Pride keeps us in the dark about the truth. Don't let pride rule your spirit. Humble yourself before God and before others and put an end to being defensive. Greet constructive criticism with an open mind. To grow spiritually, relationally, emotionally, and artistically, we need to remain open to the truth about ourselves.

Follow-Up Questions for Group Discussion

1. How do you best receive feedback?
2. What stands out to you in this chapter regarding the dangers of defensiveness?
3. Why is defensiveness such a blind spot for people?
4. What, in your opinion, causes an artist to be defensive?
5. What advice do you have for someone who struggles with defensiveness?
6. How does a defensive spirit affect a team's ability to function optimally?
7. Have you known any defensive people in your life? How did their defensiveness affect you?
8. What ground rules for critiquing would you suggest for your team?

PERSONAL ACTION STEPS

1. Rate yourself in your ability to take suggestions and in your openness to constructive criticism. Do you take offense easily, do you rarely give it a second thought, or do you fall somewhere in between?

2. Think about how others would rate you in your ability to take suggestions and be open to constructive criticism. Ask those close to you whether they feel comfortable speaking truth to you.

3. Invite feedback from three people regarding your work and consider how you can respond to each of them with grace. Make sure they're people who will be honest with you.

4. If you have received any constructive criticism recently, write down the lessons you can learn from it.

CHAPTER 6

JEALOUSY AND ENVY

SARAH LOVES TO DANCE. SHE'S BEEN dancing since she started walking, has danced professionally, and teaches at a dance studio. Sarah is also a committed Christian and has a vision for dance in worship. Every Sunday, she sits through the service dreaming about the various ways dance could be used at her church.

Sarah's efforts to launch a dance ministry at the church have been frustrating. When she first brought it up, the pastor was receptive but cautious. He and Sarah drew up a proposal and presented it to the elders. After six months of deliberation, the elders signed off on the idea but with strict guidelines. They wanted to view the dance before the service and approve the clothes Sarah and the other dancers would wear. That seemed fair enough to Sarah. She was elated to be given the green light. The pastor promised to call Sarah so they could schedule a service for the debut of the dance ministry.

Sarah never heard back from him. Special worship services came and went, as did Christmas and Easter, and still no word from anybody at church about incorporating dance. Sarah didn't know what was going on. Had she said something that offended someone? Was there something about her they didn't like? Did they change their minds about a dance ministry?

Then something strange happened. One Sunday morning the pastor got up and introduced a handsome young couple, Zach and Mariah, who had just started coming to the church. As soon as Sarah saw Mariah, she knew the beautiful young woman on the platform was a dancer. Her intuition proved right. The pastor told the congregation that Zach was a dentist and Mariah was a professional dancer. *Oh, good,* Sarah thought, *another dancer in the church.* Then the pastor said, "I know we've never included dance in our services, but that's changing as of today, and Mariah is going to facilitate worship this morning with dance." He went on to share Scripture verses regarding worshipful dance—verses that he and Sarah had featured in their presentation to the elders. The pastor said some of the same things Sarah had been saying for almost two years.

Mariah danced splendidly. The congregation was deeply

moved and gave her a standing ovation. Sarah had a strange mix of emotions. She was glad that dance had finally been given a chance at her church, but she was jealous of this newcomer, envious of all the accolades heaped on her.

The next several months were confusing for Sarah. Mariah performed a dance at church every week. Congregation members couldn't stop talking about her. They wanted her to start a dance ministry. The pastor called Sarah to see if she wanted to be a part of it. Sarah declined, making up some story about being too busy at home and at work. Meanwhile, Mariah's popularity continued to spread. She even got invited to dance at other churches.

Sarah tried to talk her husband into visiting other churches, but he didn't want to leave their church. Their children didn't want to leave either. Sarah felt stuck. She never introduced herself to Mariah, never spoke to her, and always avoided her at church. She envied Mariah's success and all the attention she received. Sarah couldn't help noticing that Mariah and her husband became good friends with the pastor and his wife. *Oh, that's it,* Sarah concluded. *She gets to dance because she's buddy-buddy with the pastor's wife. It's all politics, isn't it?*

Sarah started working in the nursery so she could get out of going to church and wouldn't have to watch Mariah and the other dancers perform. But even in the nursery she couldn't get away from Mariah's popularity. After the service, when people came to pick up their kids, they raved about her. "Don't you dance too, Sarah?" some would ask. "You should get up there with Mariah."

"Oh no, I'm too busy," Sarah would reply politely. "Besides, I've quit dancing." The latter wasn't entirely true, but she sure felt like quitting.

On occasion people asked Sarah what she thought of the new dance ministry. In a rather patronizing tone, she would point out some technical flaws that "only people who know anything about dance" would notice. She later regretted such catty comments, but they still came out of her from time to time.

Deep inside, Sarah is angry with the church and with God. She knows Christians are not supposed to be jealous or envious, so she never lets on to anyone how much she's hurting. She wishes desperately that she could run away.

Questions for Group Discussion

1. What would you do if you were Sarah?
2. How would you counsel Sarah to deal with her anger?
3. Do you think the pastor handled this situation very well? If not, how should he have handled it?
4. Do you think Sarah did the right thing by declining to be involved with the dance ministry under Mariah's leadership? Why or why not?

5. What lessons might God want Sarah to learn through this?

6. What lessons might God want the pastor to learn from this?

7. What lessons might God want Mariah to learn through this?

8. How common is jealousy and envy among artists in the church? Do you think it's a major problem?

Jealousy and Envy among Artists

Have you ever envied someone else's talents, abilities, or success? Have you ever been jealous of someone whose talents threatened your status or your role in the ministry? If you're an artist, you need to know how to deal with jealousy and envy, because there will always be someone more talented, more successful, or more appealing than you.

The artistic community has struggled with jealousy and envy for centuries. One dramatic example involves the Italian Renaissance painter Giovanni da San Giovanni (1592–1636), who, as a young man, moved to Rome to make a living as an artist. At the time, bitter rivalries raged among the artists in Rome. Giovanni received a commission to paint a fresco for Cardinal Bentivoglio and set out to work on it at once. After the first day of laboring on his new masterpiece, he went home. When he came back the next day, he found dirt and mold all over the painting. Giovanni thought there was something wrong with the plaster he was using, so he kept trying different mixtures. But the results were the same. Every day he'd arrive and find the previous day's work ruined. This went on for five days, until it dawned on him that this might be the work of vandals. He decided to sleep at the church so he could keep watch. Sure enough, about midnight the perpetrators broke in, and as they climbed up the scaffolding, Giovanni pushed the ladder over, sending them crashing to the floor. They turned out to be two jealous French painters in town.

Henri Nouwen writes very graphically about backstage hostility in his book *Reaching Out*. "Recently an actor told me stories about his professional world which seemed symbolic of much of our contemporary situation. While rehearsing the most moving scenes of love, tenderness and intimate relationships, the actors were so jealous of each other and so full of apprehension about their chances to 'make it,' that the back stage scene was one of hatred, harshness and mutual suspicion. Those who kissed each other on the stage were tempted to hit each other behind it, and those who portrayed the most profound human emotions of love in the footlights displayed the most trivial and hostile rivalries as soon as the footlights had dimmed."[39]

Unfortunately, relationships among artists are often characterized by a high degree of jealousy and envy.

What's the Difference between Jealousy and Envy?

The meanings of the words jealousy and envy are similar but distinct. Jealousy is the fear of losing something that belongs to you, and it typically involves a triangle of relationships (say, a husband, his wife, and another man). A jealous person agonizes over the prospect of losing to a third party what he or she already has. Jealousy has a sense of rivalry to it. A veteran musician on the worship team can feel threatened by a talented newcomer and fear losing his or her place in the ministry.

Envy occurs over something you want that someone else has, such as talent, popularity, or attention, so it involves two people. Someone on the tech team could envy the person behind the soundboard because that's the job he or she wanted for themself.

Thou Shalt Not Covet

In the eyes of God, jealousy and envy are serious sins. Aaron and Miriam were envious of their brother Moses' special relationship with God, and Miriam was struck with leprosy, which put her in isolation for seven days (Num. 12:1–15). This sibling rivalry threatened the fragile unity of God's people. Facing a similar threat, Paul confronted the Corinthians about the jealousy that was tearing them apart (1 Cor. 3:3; 2 Cor. 12:20). He considered the sin of jealousy to be as serious as carousing, drunkenness, and sexual promiscuity (Rom. 13:13). James tells us that wherever there's envy and selfish ambition, "there you find disorder and every evil practice" (3:16). Matthew says that the reason the religious leaders crucified Jesus was because they envied him (27:18 NASB).

Jealousy and envy are more common among artists in the church than we care to admit. As we serve the Lord together, there is always the potential for jealousy and envy. The very first murder was committed by a man who envied his own brother to death, so to speak. Even worse, Cain's lethal envy arose as the two brothers were trying to serve God as an act of worship (Genesis 4). Human envy can ruin our attempts to serve peacefully together in worship.

Dealing With the Green-Eyed Monster

I began teaching on this topic because I saw in myself and in the artists I led an inability to deal with jealousy and envy in a healthy way. There seems to be an ambivalence around this issue, a reluctance even to talk about it. After all, everyone knows it's wrong for Christians to covet, right? It violates the Ten Commandments (Ex. 20:17). But instead of owning our covetousness, we minimize it or suppress it, which only causes it to come out sideways, usually as anger. We get upset because someone else gets to sing lead. We're offended because we feel we're being treated unfairly. We become territorial because we're afraid of losing our vaunted position in the ministry. We might gossip or slander, spread rumors about our rival, or put him or her down. Sometimes the anger turns passive-aggressive. We can't bring ourselves to root for our competitor. Instead of wishing that person success, we secretly wish that he or she fails. We're unable to "rejoice with those who rejoice" (Rom. 12:15). The poet Dante writes from the perspective of a man who was so envious of someone that he couldn't tolerate the prospect of good things happening to that person.

> The fires of envy raged so in my blood
> that I turned livid if I chanced to see
> another man rejoice in his own good.[40]

Working with artists in the church, I've too often seen Christians deal with jealousy and envy by turning against themselves. We know it's not right for "good Christians" to be envious, so we redirect inward the contempt we feel for someone else, by devaluing our own talents and abilities. *I'm not as good as so-and-so,* we conclude, *so why even try anymore?* Covetousness is often the root of such self-deprecating statements.

Galatians 5:26 tells us not to envy one another. First Peter 2:1 instructs us to put all envy aside. How do we do that? Jealousy and envy are strong feelings that don't easily go away. Proverbs 27:4 stresses that "anger is cruel and fury overwhelming, but who can stand before jealousy?" How can we rid ourselves of something so formidable as jealousy or envy? Let's talk about some ways we can cooperate with God's efforts to work in our hearts and help us love one another instead of compete against each other.

CONFESS IT AS SIN

The first step to being free from jealousy and envy is to confess it as sin. Stop justifying it, excusing it, or tolerating it. Own up to your jealousy or envy and confess it before the Lord. James 3:14 warns against harboring "bitter envy and selfish ambition" in our hearts, reveling in them, or denying the truth. God knows your every thought, so he's not going to be surprised by your confession. Ask him to help you deal with this issue.

STOP COMPARING

Nothing good comes from comparing ourselves with others. We end up looking either better than we really are or worse than we really are. The danger of comparing, according to Paul, is that it makes us vulnerable to jealousy and envy. "If the foot should say, 'Because I am not a hand, I do not belong to the body,' it would not for that reason stop being part of the body. And if the ear should say, 'Because I am not an eye, I do not belong to the body,' it would not for that reason stop being part of the body" (1 Cor. 12:15–16). Comparison causes us to judge the validity of our gifts as well as the gifts of others.

Gordon MacDonald writes that "the soul cannot be healthy when one compares himself or herself to others. The soul dies a bit every time it is involved in a lifestyle that competes. It gives way to the destructive forces of rivalry, envy, and jealousy."[41] When we stop comparing, we stop competing. Only then can we become secure in our giftedness. We realize that God isn't asking us to be like someone else or to be as talented or accomplished as some other artist. He's inviting us to grow in our unique abilities, to be as talented and accomplished as we can be. When we stop comparing ourselves with others, we can discover the unique role God has for us and fulfill it with enthusiasm. We will always be more content by being who God made us to be than by trying to be someone else.

Some men asked John the Baptist how he felt about the large crowds that Jesus was attracting. People who had been following John were now following Jesus. Was John envious of all the attention Jesus was getting? No, because first, John knew that he himself was not the Messiah. "I am not the Messiah," he said, "but am sent ahead of him" (John 3:28). John was well aware of his limits. He had no illusions about his place in the world. Second, John was secure in who he was and what God called him to do. He saw himself as the friend of Jesus, as the best man at a wedding, standing beside the bridegroom, rejoicing for him, not drawing attention to himself but pointing everyone to Jesus. John was content to be what God made him to be—no more, no less. Refusing to compare yourself with others can free you from the unrealistic expectation to be someone you're not.

APPRECIATE YOUR GOD-GIVEN TALENT

Be thankful for whatever talent the Lord has given you. First Peter 4:10 confirms that each of us has received a special gift from God. Your talent is a gift from the Lord. Romans 12:6 adds that "God has given each of us the ability to do certain things well" (TLB). What ability has God given you? Acknowledge that and be grateful for it. When we envy somebody else's talents, we forget about all that God has given us.

I knew a keyboard player who was discouraged because his songwriting wasn't taking off the way he wanted it to. He said he didn't want to be known as just a piano player. It's a shame because he was one of the best keyboard players I've ever worked with. I know people who would give their eyeteeth to play like he could. If you have an artistic ability—you paint, act, dance, write, do graphic design—you can do something that the average human being cannot. Appreciate that talent God has so graciously gifted you.

DEVELOP RELATIONSHIPS INSTEAD OF RIVALRIES

We tend to alienate ourselves from those we envy. We hold them at arm's length and view them as enemies. Bitter rivalries between artists may be common, even acceptable, in the entertainment industry, but they have no place among artists in the church. Instead of building walls, we should build bridges with our teammates, especially those who might otherwise be our competitors. Stop viewing them as your competition and begin treating them as friends.

The Bible tells the story of two young men, David and Jonathan, who instead of being archrivals became loyal friends. Jonathan had every reason to be jealous of David. As heir to the throne, Jonathan was next in line to be king, yet God had anointed David to reign. Jonathan chose to be David's friend instead of his adversary, and their souls became knit together in friendship (1 Sam. 18:1).

Like David and Jonathan, we too need to develop friendships, not rivalries. Instead of withdrawing from those we envy, we need to move toward them in love. I discovered that spending time with potential rivals enabled me to relate to them and know them as people, not competitors. The more I got to know them, the less threatening they became. I found myself praying for them, even praying for their success. You won't remain jealous or envious of your fellow artists if you're praying for them and building relationships with them.

TURN ENVY INTO WORSHIP

Once upon a time, there was a bandleader who was lining up musicians for a gig at a jazz club. He hired the best trio he could find and promised to pay them union scale. The trio's opening set sounded fantastic. They brought down the house. During the break, the bandleader decided to hire a couple of horn players, and they arrived in time for the band's second set. The chemistry among the musicians was electric. Again the crowd cheered wildly. The bandleader then called in a singer to join the band for the third set. At the end of the night, the bandleader gathered backstage with his musicians and handed out the paychecks. Some of them got angry when they discovered that everyone received the same amount of money. The trio was especially upset. They had shouldered more of the workload than the others but were paid the same amount. Tempers flared and tensions mounted. The bandleader finally spoke up. "Is your check incorrect?" he asked. "Is it not the amount we agreed on?"

"Yeah, but I thought we'd get more," complained the drummer. "We played the whole night. We deserve more than the others."

"That's right," shouted the piano player. "It isn't fair!"

The bandleader was firm. "I haven't cheated you out of anything. Can't I do what I want with my money? Or are you envious because I'm generous?"

The preceding story is an adaptation of Jesus' parable about the workers in the vineyard (Matthew 20). The bandleader's final question—"Are you envious because I am generous?" (v. 15)—makes me realize that my concept of what's fair is too limiting for a gracious God like ours. I want God to distribute gifts and talents as I would if I were him (perish the thought), but God is much more giving and far more gracious than I. He distributes gifts to each of us according to his perfect will (1 Cor. 12:11).

Acknowledging God's sovereignty in the way he distributes gifts and abilities enables us to turn envy into worship. We can praise God for the talents he's given us, and we can also praise the Lord for the talents he's bestowed on others. Instead of envying someone or feeling threatened by another artist, I can thank God for how he's gifted that brother or sister.

Free from Jealousy and Envy

When we confess our sin, stop comparing ourselves with others, appreciate our God-given talents, develop relationships instead of rivalries, and turn envy into worship, we will no longer be threatened by another artist's talents and abilities. We will be secure in who we are and more concerned with being faithful than with being successful.

BE SECURE IN WHO YOU ARE

Those who are free from jealousy and envy are secure about who they are as artists created in the image of God, saved by the blood of Christ, and anointed by the Holy Spirit. Such artists do not go into a tailspin when a colleague succeeds; they know that the accomplishments of other artists do not steal anything from them. The secure artist is not threatened by someone else's achievements.

Numbers 11 records the story of two men who were prophesying mightily before the people of Israel. Joshua took offense for Moses. He wanted these men stopped because they were taking the limelight away from Moses. Joshua brought the matter to Moses, demanding that he do something to stop these false prophets (v. 28). Moses, however, was a wise man who was not threatened by the gifts of others. He responded to Joshua with a question. "Are you jealous for my sake? I wish that all the LORD's people were prophets and that the LORD would put his Spirit on them!" (v. 29). Moses realized that he didn't have a monopoly on the gift of prophecy. He was secure in his giftedness and in his calling. He saw a need for more prophets, and he cared more for the kingdom of God than for his own glory.

Like Moses, we need not be threatened by the talents of others. We can rejoice when God elevates a fellow artist.

Instead of withholding approval, we can applaud their success, give credit where credit is due, and encourage them in their work.

BE A FAITHFUL STEWARD

I've always loved Jesus' parable of the talents (Matthew 25). The story about the man entrusting his possessions to his servants while he's away reminds me that God has entrusted me with artistic gifts. My job is to steward them. One thing that used to bother me about this passage, though, was the disparity between the number of talents. I wondered why one person was given five talents, another two, and another only one. It doesn't seem fair, does it? Shouldn't they all have been given the same amount? The Bible assures us that our God is a righteous God; everything he does is right. He knows what he's doing. The man in the parable entrusted each servant "according to his ability" (v. 15). Romans 12:6 also suggests that gifts and abilities are given out not equally but in proportions.

I can't tell you why one person is given five talents, another two, and some of us only one. Life is like that, it seems. Some have been granted prodigious amounts of talents, while others have been modestly blessed. The real issue is not who gets what or how much we get but whether you and I faithfully steward what God has entrusted to us. We are not called to be successful or famous; we are called to be faithful and obedient. Spiritually mature artists view themselves as faithful stewards of the talents God gave them.

If You've Got It, Don't Flaunt It

What if you're the object of someone else's jealousy or envy? If you find yourself in that situation, can I suggest that you be sensitive to the one who's struggling? First Peter 5:3 warns against being domineering or using our giftedness to lord it over others, so be careful not to flaunt your talents and abilities or rub your success in the faces of those struggling with jealousy and envy. After all, you never want to cause a brother or sister to stumble (1 Cor. 8:13).

The Old Testament story of Joseph and his brothers is marked by bitter resentment and cruel envy. Jacob favored Joseph above all his other sons. The brothers, therefore, were seething with envy toward little Joe. So it didn't help family dynamics when Jacob gave his favorite son a specially made, multicolored robe. Joseph's relationship with his brothers was further strained when he predicted that someday they would bow down in submission to him (Gen. 37:6–11). No wonder they didn't like him; he was cocky. The brothers already felt ignored by their dad. They didn't need this little whippersnapper to keep reminding them about it. I know Joseph couldn't help being the object of his father's favor, but I wonder how different his relationship with his brothers would have been if he had shown more discretion. If you've been given mega talent, don't walk around with a mega ego. Don't flaunt your abilities. People who are secure in who they are don't need to keep propping themselves up all the time.

Follow-Up Questions for Group Discussion

1. What would make it hard for artists to talk about feelings of jealousy or envy they might have toward another artist?
2. Do you think the Christian community does an adequate job of addressing the problem of jealousy and envy? Why or why not?
3. Have you ever seen a relationship strained or ended by jealousy or envy? What was that like?
4. What do you think prevents us from being content with the talents we've been given?
5. In what ways could healthy competition benefit an artistic community? When is competition bad for a team of artists?
6. Which of the five suggestions for dealing with jealousy and envy—confess it as sin, stop comparing, appreciate your God-given talents, develop relationships instead of rivalries, turn envy into worship—do you feel is most important?
7. How can people with similar gifts and talents cultivate friendship?

PERSONAL ACTION STEPS

1. Confess any jealousy or envy you're harboring toward a fellow artist and ask the Lord to help you deal with this issue.
2. Identify any tendencies you have to compare yourself with other artists.
3. Thank the Lord for the talents he's given you.
4. Come up with three things you can do to cultivate a healthy relationship with someone who might otherwise be your rival.
5. Find a way to express your praise for and gratitude to God for the way he distributes gifts and talents.

CHAPTER 7

MANAGING YOUR EMOTIONS

DAN IS WHAT SOME PEOPLE CALL a real artist. He's a twenty-year-old student at the Art Institute of Chicago, and he hopes to make a living someday as an artist. Dan's favorite medium is pencil, and he carries around a pocket-size sketchbook everywhere he goes. He's consumed with his work and will forgo food or sleep when focused on a project.

With such all-out dedication to his art, Dan doesn't have much time for a social life or extracurricular activities. His only social outlet is a weekly small group at church, which has been meeting for about a year. But Dan is starting to wonder whether he should continue in the group. He feels out of step with everyone else. He's often perceived as moody because he wears his emotions on his sleeve. He can be painfully honest, sometimes to a fault.

Take last week's meeting at the home of Ted and Nancy Jones. Ted and Nancy were high school sweethearts. He was an all-state football standout, and Nancy was a cheerleader. Ted had asked everyone to come to the meeting having selected a psalm that best describes where his or her life is at right now. Ted is in seminary, studying to be a pastor. He selected Psalm 1:1 and read it as if he were giving a sermon. "Blessed is the one who does not walk in step with the wicked or stand in the way that sinners take or sit in the company of mockers." He had just finished writing a paper on that passage, so it was fresh in his mind. Nancy went next and proceeded to celebrate how God had recently blessed her and Ted financially. She enthusiastically read Psalm 100:5. "The LORD is good and his love endures forever; his faithfulness continues through all generations." Adele Peterson was next. She's a nurse. Ted and Nancy have been trying to match her up with Dan. She's also been struggling in a new job and shared a passage about trusting God, Psalm 37:4–5. "Take delight in the LORD, and he will give you the desires of your heart. Commit your way to the LORD; trust in him and he will do this."

Then it was Dan's turn. He nervously thumbed through his Bible, muttering to himself. Eventually he began talking about being discouraged, but he wasn't sure why he felt that way. "I can't put a finger on it," he tried to explain. "I had an argument with my dad; maybe that has something to do with it. Although, my rent's overdue again; that could be it too." He also mentioned that he's tired of the cold, gray Chicago winters that linger too long into spring.

The more Dan talked, the more he rambled. He was struggling to put thoughts together and growing increasingly frustrated because he couldn't put into words what he was feeling. He finally cut off midsentence and read Psalm 88, starting with verse 13. "I cry to you for help, LORD; in the morning my prayer comes before you. Why, LORD, do you reject me and hide your face from me? From my youth I have suffered and been close to death; I have borne your terrors and am in despair. Your wrath has swept over me; your terrors have destroyed me. All day long they surround me like a flood; they have completely engulfed me. You have taken from me friend and neighbor—darkness is my closest friend."

There was an uneasy silence when Dan finished. Ted cleared his throat before speaking. "Why, Dan, with all the blessings God has given, I was hoping you would read something uplifting, like one of the praise psalms. Psalm 150, perhaps?"

Dan didn't know what to say. He was kicking himself for sharing as much as he had, yet he was just being honest. Nancy tried to break the tension with humor. "Sounds like it's time to break out the refreshments. That should cheer us all up." Adele giggled. There was good-natured laughter and chuckles all around the room, except from where Dan sat. He didn't engage much with the group the rest of the night. He shut down and withdrew inside himself. He left early with the excuse that he had to get up early in the morning for class.

Questions for Group Discussion

1. Do you approve of how the small group reacted to Dan's sharing? If not, how do you think they should have responded?
2. Do you think Dan had good reason to be down, or was he just being moody?
3. Have you ever experienced anything similar to what happened to Dan? What was that like for you?
4. Dan could have suppressed his feelings and shared something a lot safer. Do you think that would have been a good idea? Why or why not?
5. What challenges await those who wear their emotions on their sleeve?
6. How do you react to someone who's predominantly negative, critical, or moody?
7. How can you tell if you're being controlled by your emotions?

Emotions: Friend or Foe?

Many of us with artistic temperaments are more emotional, more in touch with our feelings, than other people. I believe that the ability to experience emotions is a wonderful privilege, but I didn't always think of feelings in a positive light. As I was growing up, I somehow got the message that it wasn't proper for a man to show emotion. Men weren't supposed to cry or be overly exuberant. They were to be stable, meaning emotionless. As a result, I suppressed a lot of feelings. When I became a Christian, though, the door cracked open a bit. I noticed that Jesus wept (Luke 19:41; John 11:35), as did Paul (Acts 20:19). Ecclesiastes speaks of "a time to weep and a time to laugh" (3:4). So emotions seemed to be okay with God.

When I got married, the door opened even farther as my ever-patient wife gently prodded me to engage emotionally with her. In the process, I discovered feelings I never knew I had. But the greatest emotional emancipation occurred when I became a father. Being there when both my boys were born was just the starting point of all the intense feelings I've had, and always will have, for them. Because of this emotional evolution, I enjoy a great deal of emotional freedom. I tend to be passionate and feel things deeply.

This emotional freedom can quickly turn to bondage if I'm not careful, though. When people talk about the tortured artist, they're usually referring to the propensity we artists have to be controlled by our emotions. The great Italian opera composer Giacomo Puccini is known to have said that he always carried "a great sack of melancholy."[42] At its worst, such melancholy can result in serious mental and emotional disorders. Examples of artists suffering such maladies have been well documented throughout history. At the age of twenty-two, Michelangelo wrote in a letter to his father, "Do not wonder if I have sometimes written irritable letters, for I often suffer great distresses of mind and temper."[43] Berlioz, Tchaikovsky, and Rachmaninoff all experienced severe depression. Robert Schumann and Hugo Wolf were manic-depressive. Songwriter Jimmy Webb says this about the artist's frequent bouts with depression: "The true poet understands this strange mood shift all too well—walking out the front door onto the porch on a glorious spring morning, serenaded by the liquid songs of birds, only to find that the day has taken on a darkly sinister aspect and that there is a uranium slug suddenly buried in the pit of the stomach—all made worse by the fact the victim knows all too well that the cause lies within. . . . The effort involved in holding this monster at bay creates other vulnerabilities: the temptation to self-medicate along with the addictions that may follow, as well as related professional failures that may destroy a person's faith in their own future."[44] If you struggle with your emotions, my artistic friend, you are in good company.

I often get calls from pastors because the worship leader they're thinking about hiring listed me as a reference, so they want my opinion of the candidate. During the conversation, pastors often ask me whether the person is moody, overly critical, or negative. Apparently, no one wants to hire a worship leader who brings everyone down because he or she always has the blues. My hope is that we artists will be free to be who God made us to be as emotional human beings but not be controlled by our emotions. I pray that we be emotionally healthy—in touch with our feelings but not enslaved by them.

At the outset, I need to emphasize that if you're continually depressed or you're entertaining thoughts of suicide or other destructive behavior, you need to seek professional help from a Christian counselor or pastor. Clinical depression warrants professional and sometimes medical attention. Please get the help you need.

Is It Okay to Be Sad?

Some people have grown up with the idea that negative emotions such as anger, disappointment, and sadness are unacceptable, especially for Christians. The thinking here is that being down or depressed would be a bad witness to our unsaved friends. So they suppress their feelings, thinking God (and the neighbors) can't handle their sadness or grief.

God has certainly proven that he can handle our darkest emotions. The Old Testament prophet Elijah was so distraught he wanted to die (1 Kings 19:4). Jeremiah was so despondent he cursed the day he was born (Jer. 20:14–15). God didn't turn his back on these men when they were weak. Scripture affirms that God draws near to the brokenhearted and "saves those who are crushed in spirit" (Ps. 34:18). There's even an entire book of the Bible called Lamentations. God can handle it when we're sad and depressed. Jesus regards as blessed those who mourn (Matt. 5:4). Rather than have us avoid our pain and suffering, God invites us to embrace them.

Since God receives with open arms those who mourn, we—his church—need to open our hearts to those who are downcast. Paul instructs us to "encourage the fainthearted, help the weak, be patient with everyone" (1 Thess. 5:14 NASB). We are to "mourn with those who mourn" (Rom. 12:15). Church should be a place where people can be honest about how they feel.

Veteran Christians sometimes go through what Saint John of the Cross refers to as "the dark night of the soul," which is a prolonged period of sadness and spiritual deadness. Richard Foster sees this dark night as something God uses for various reasons, one of which is to break us of a faith that's based mostly on our feelings. During this dark night of the soul, Foster writes, we "may have a sense of dryness, aloneness, even lostness. Any overdependence on the emotional life is stripped away. The notion, often heard today, that such experiences should be avoided and that we always should live in peace and comfort, joy, and celebration only betrays the fact that much contemporary experience is surface slush. The dark night is one of the ways God brings us into a hush, a stillness, so that he may work an inner transformation upon the soul."[45] God can use negative emotions to transform us and draw us closer to him.

When Our Emotions Get the Best of Us

Feelings are good; they're one of an artist's vital strengths. But if you let them control you, they can be a liability. If you allow yourself to be ruled by your emotions, you will make bad decisions, you'll misread circumstances, and you'll end up out of touch with reality.

How do you know whether you're being controlled by your emotions? If you know something is true but act like it's not, you're letting your emotions get the best of you. If you know you're qualified for the job but you hang back because you feel inadequate, if you know God loves you but you feel insecure all the time, if you know that relationship is unhealthy but you can't bring yourself to end it, you're being controlled by your emotions. If people often refer to you as moody or describe you as being on an emotional roller coaster, that's a dead giveaway that your emotions are dictating your life.

People who don't know how to manage their emotions tend to base their feelings about God on how they feel about themselves. If their lives are going well, God must like them. If things aren't going well, God must be mad at them. If they don't feel God's presence, God has abandoned them. Being controlled by our emotions can be just as unhealthy as suppressing them.

Managing Our Emotions

The writer of Proverbs likens someone lacking self-control to a city whose walls are broken down (25:28). The person who doesn't know how to manage his or her emotions is defenseless against negative feelings. Proverbs 16:32 adds that the person who manages his or her emotions well is better than someone who captures an entire city. It's easier to conquer a city than to conquer negative emotions.

Managing our emotions is one of the most difficult challenges facing those of us with artistic temperaments. When I'm hurt, it can trigger a chain reaction of emotions that causes me to say or do something I later regret. I end up wishing I had kept my wits about me and used my head instead of responding emotionally. It's not easy for emotional people like us to avoid being controlled by our feelings. Let's consider some ways to manage our emotions so they don't manage us.

BE PROACTIVE ABOUT TRUTH

First, we could stand to be more objective about our feelings. Instead of being pulled unquestioningly by our emotions, we need to evaluate them, to examine them in light of the truth. Just because you feel a certain way doesn't mean what you're feeling is true. Perhaps it's how you truly feel, but it could still be a lie. Be willing to say, "Even though I feel this way, it might not reflect accurately or completely what's really going on."

We don't always have to react according to how we feel; we can choose a different response. Next time you catch yourself jumping to a negative conclusion, stop to ask yourself whether the information that led you there is accurate. Or did you make assumptions en route to that conclusion? Next time you catch yourself assuming the worst of someone or some situation, ask yourself whether you're basing your reaction on truth or speculation. Commit to believe the best about people and their interactions with you. Be proactive about the truth; don't always assume or insist that what you're feeling is true to the situation at hand. It might not be.

Paul instructs us to dwell on "whatever is true" (Phil. 4:8)—to let God's Word permeate our hearts and minds so it can change the way we think (Rom. 12:2). Ecclesiastes 8:1

says that God's Word can settle into someone who's angry or sad and cause their "face to beam" (NASB). Reading the Bible regularly can keep our hearts aligned with God's truth.

THROW YOURSELF INTO WORSHIP

To avoid being controlled by your feelings, channel them into worship. Worship helps us to be proactive about truth—spiritual truth. John Piper explains the role of truth and emotion as it relates to worship: "Truth without emotion produces dead orthodoxy and a church full (or half full) of artificial admirers (like people who write generic anniversary cards for a living). Emotion without truth produces empty frenzy and cultivates shallow people who refuse the disciplines of rigorous thought. But true worship comes from people who are deeply emotional and who love deep and sound doctrine. Strong affections from God rooted in truth are the bone and marrow of biblical worship."[46]

Worship not only enables us to express our feelings (positive and negative), it offers God's perspective on those feelings. William Temple defines worship as "the submission of all our nature to God. It is the quickening of conscience by his holiness; the nourishment of mind with his truth; the purifying of imagination by his beauty; the opening of the heart to his love; the surrender of will to his purpose—and all of this gathered up in adoration, the most selfless emotion of which our nature is capable and therefore the chief remedy for that self-centeredness which is our original sin and the source of all actual sin."[47]

Did you catch Temple's line about worship expressing selfless emotion? When we connect with God in heartfelt worship, we realize that this life is not all about us. It's about the Lord. By taking the focus off ourselves and putting it on him, worship puts our feelings in the context of who God is. Worship doesn't solve all our problems or make them go away. But our problems look different in light of who God is. Worship can prevent our feelings from taking over our lives and enable us to keep our emotions in balance.

When Saul struggled emotionally, he asked David to play the harp for him. Knowing David, I bet he didn't play dinner music all night. I'm sure he threw in a lot of praise choruses. First Samuel 16:23 reports that David's music ministered to Saul and refreshed him. Worship can transform our moods and attitudes, which is why C. S. Lewis referred to worship as "inner health made audible."[48] By helping us establish emotional equilibrium and keeping God's truth at the forefront, worship can be a healthy and productive outlet for our emotions.

For the longest time I couldn't relate to the word magnify during worship. I could relate to words like bless, exalt, and extol, but magnify had me stumped. What does it mean to magnify the Lord? Then it hit me that when problems come into my life, I usually magnify them to the point where they're bigger than God is. We artists have a tendency to magnify everything in our lives—our problems, our emotions, and even our art—until they're bigger than God. Now when I hear or sing "magnify the Lord," I take that as an invitation to throw myself into worshiping the God who is bigger than any problem that comes my way.

DON'T TAKE YOURSELF TOO SERIOUSLY

Sometimes we can be too serious for our own good. I know I tend to take myself too seriously. In his eternal wisdom, God gave me a wife who likes to laugh. Sue has a great sense of humor. It's one of the traits that attracted me to her. I love being around her, because she laughs easily. Laughter is heard frequently at our house. Sue would tell you it's one of the keys to a successful marriage. I know firsthand what Scripture means when it says that "a cheerful heart is good medicine" (Prov. 17:22). Laughter can help balance our emotions.

God certainly has a sense of humor. Did you know that the male seahorse is the one who gives birth? I bet God laughed hysterically when he came up with that idea. Jesus was a master at mixing humorous anecdotes into his teaching. The image of a man trying to remove a speck of sawdust from someone's eye with a gigantic plank sticking out of his own eye is quite funny. I bet the disciples laughed when they heard it. Or the one about a camel going through the eye of a needle. We read these stories with a straight face, but I imagine Jesus chuckling as he told them. I bet he had to stop a few times until the disciples' laughter subsided. Christians who are too religious to have any fun or too serious to laugh are missing out on the joy of living. Joy is one of the fruits of the Spirit, and laughter is indeed good for the soul. The writer of Ecclesiastes warns against being overly righteous or overly wise (7:16). Don't take everything (including yourself) so seriously that you can no longer laugh, smile, or enjoy life.

BRING YOUR SADNESS TO GOD

It's easier to be proactive about truth, throw ourselves into worship, and retain a sense of humor when things are going well. How about when things are not going so well? Throughout the Psalms, we see the writers, all of whom were poets or songwriters, bringing their pain and sorrow to God. Never one to gloss over his true feelings, David prays, "Turn to me and be gracious to me, for I am lonely and afflicted. Relieve the troubles of my heart and free me from my anguish" (Ps. 25:16–17). The psalmists were emotional, sensitive human beings (like us) struggling with the difficulties of life, but they kept bringing their frustrations to God. They were honest with the Lord about how they felt and didn't hold back their negative thoughts and feelings. We would do well to follow their example. Bring God all your sadness, all your despair, all your disappointments.

Dealing With Disappointment

Artists tend to be well acquainted with disappointment. Life always seems to come up short, and people always seem to let us down. We're not only easily disappointed but also tend to internalize it, even wallow in it. How do you handle disappointment? Do you hold grudges? Do you harbor anger and bitterness? Or do you turn your anger inward and become depressed?

Many of us start out with dreams of making it as an artist, but that ambition is not always realized. Some people are fortunate enough to make a living in the arts; others are not. You may be more talented than those successful artists, but you never got the breaks they did. A career in the arts hasn't happened for you. How have you handled the fact that your hopes and dreams never materialized?

What if you've been disappointed by the church? What happens if you experience rejection in your place of worship? Or if your church doesn't use your gifts the way you think they should? What if using your talents at church turns out to be far from the fulfilling experience you hoped it would be?

Anybody who plays tennis knows that when you serve, the best place to make contact with the ball is dead center in the middle of the racket. When the ball hits that sweet spot, it jumps off the racket and shoots straight over the net. It would be nice if all artists could serve in their sweet spot all the time. But that's not a realistic expectation, and things don't always work out that way. Our talents don't always get used to their full potential. I'm thinking about the serious writer who wants to do more than write copy for the church bulletin, or the visual artist who wants to do more than make banners at Easter. What if you write songs but they never get played at church? Negotiating such disappointments can be a challenge.

SHOULD I GO OR SHOULD I STAY?

Artists who become disenchanted with their church often wonder whether they should find another place to worship. In those cases, caution is advised. Leaving your church is a big decision, so make sure you seek direction from the Lord. Don't leave unless you sense God releasing you to go. Make sure you're not running away from your problems and that you're not being stubborn or prideful. If God is definitely calling you to leave, make sure you do so graciously. Don't burn bridges, don't leave angry, and don't take parting shots at leadership as you head out the door.

God may call you to stay instead of leave, even though it's frustrating. The Lord may have you there for a reason you can't see right now. Who knows? Your situation might improve over the coming months. You or your ministry could be on the verge of some major breakthroughs that seem impossible today. The Israelites were surrounded by enemies and outnumbered when Joshua predicted that the Lord was going to do "amazing things" among them (Josh. 3:5). Yet that's exactly what God did. If God is about to do something amazing with you or at your church, you would miss it if you left. Our toil in the Lord is never in vain (1 Cor. 15:58).

IS IT TIME FOR A CHAT?

What if what stands in the way of your being fulfilled as an artist in the church is a person? Is your leader not scheduling you to play or sing? Are you and your leader not getting along these days? It might be time for you both to sit down and talk. If so, I suggest you schedule that meeting sooner rather than later. I've always believed that my volunteers deserve to know how I view their role and their place in the ministry. They deserve to know why I deal with them the way I do. I'm guessing that your leader would welcome a conversation with you about your ministry at the church.

When you meet, be careful not to come across as angry or vindictive. Be humble, respectful, and polite. Simply share, as lovingly as you can, your frustration. Your leader might be unaware of your situation. You might discover that the reason you're not being used has nothing to do with you at all. Or you might learn that there are some things, such as certain skills, holding you back. Be open to what your leader has to say. Whatever it is, you will come away from that meeting knowing exactly where you stand.

WAIT ON THE LORD'S TIMING

It may be that God has not elevated you to that role or leadership position you aspire to because you're not quite ready for it. God is the one who raises up people to serve (Ps. 75:7). He exalts us "at the proper time" (1 Peter 5:6 NASB). Is it possible that now is not the proper time for you? The Lord may have you in a season of preparation when you can hone your skills and grow spiritually. God may be inviting you to wait on his perfect timing.

Waiting is never easy. We tend to seek instant gratification in all things. God promised the Israelites that they would subdue the city of Jericho, but it involved an unconventional battle strategy. For six days they were to march around Jericho once without saying a word and then return to camp. At first it must have been a real hoot to get all dressed up and take a lap around Jericho. But I imagine it got old quickly. I'm sure some of them must have thought, *What are we waiting for? We know God is in this, so why do we have to wait another day?* I bet those trumpet players were getting impatient waiting to blow their horns. On the seventh day the Israelites marched around the city seven times, until Joshua gave them the command to blow the trumpets and shout. We all know what happened next. The walls came a-tumblin' down. Just like the people of Israel, you may have to wait until the time is right for you and your ministry, at which point your obstacles will be removed. Those walls will crumble.

The prophet Isaiah proclaimed that "those who wait for the LORD will gain new strength; they will mount up with wings like eagles, they will run and not get tired, they will walk and not become weary" (Isa. 40:31 NASB). Waiting produces strength to endure and courage to carry on. While we wait, God brings spiritual growth into our lives. We grow in faith, trusting that the plans God has for us are for our welfare and not for our calamity, that they offer us a bright future and an enduring hope (Jer. 29:11). We also learn to persevere, because we are convinced that "in all things God works for the good of those who love him, who have been called according to his purpose" (Rom. 8:28). We can be at peace, therefore, about God's timing. Even when it doesn't feel right to us, we realize that his timing is always perfect.

Learning to Be Content

As we learn to manage our emotions and deal with our disappointment, we eventually become content in all circumstances, able to maintain our equilibrium through the ups and downs of life. Paul emerged from the adversities of life and found contentment. According to 2 Corinthians 11, he endured imprisonment, physical abuse, danger, and starvation. Yet he learned to be content in all things (Phil. 4:11).

No wonder he said that "godliness with contentment is great gain" (1 Tim. 6:6). Paul was content because he was at peace with himself and with God (1 Tim. 6:8; Heb. 13:5).

Discontentment causes us to forget how much God has done for us (1 Tim. 6:7–8). Paul reminds the Christians at Galatia of their initial gratitude for the gospel, and then cries out to them, "Where then is that sense of blessing you had?" (Gal. 4:13–15 NASB). Discontent robs us of our sense of blessedness and makes us ungrateful. Contentment, on the other hand, allows us to see what we want in light of what we have. We stop insisting we need what we don't really need. We stop demanding that all our problems be solved. And we don't need to get our way all the time. We realize we don't deserve what we already have, let alone anything more. Our joy doesn't depend on outward things or circumstances, because we've already been blessed with God's amazing grace.

PRACTICE GRATITUDE

Gratitude, then, is the key to contentment. I can't help but notice that the worship leaders in the Bible are explicitly tasked with giving thanks to God (2 Chron. 20:21). The first organized choir in the Bible was formed to lead others in giving thanks (1 Chron. 16:7–36). Nehemiah gives the impression that the only type of music he allowed his choir to sing was hymns of thanksgiving (Neh. 12:8, 27, 46). Isn't it interesting that the people who struggle most with negativity and cynicism are the ones responsible for leading worshipers every week in praise and thanksgiving?

For those of us who lead worship, practicing gratitude is a job requirement. "Give thanks in all circumstances," Scripture says (1 Thess. 5:18). To grow in gratitude, I recommend identifying three things you're grateful for every day—blessings, answered prayers, people, and so on. Then thank God verbally for each one. Don't make this merely an intellectual exercise. Don't name three reasons to be thankful and then move on with your day. Take the time to articulate your gratitude. Give God your heartfelt thanks. My fellow artists, let's never lose our sense of blessing. Cultivate gratitude in your life.

BE CAREFUL HOW YOU MEASURE SUCCESS

You could release a worship recording and be famous the world over and still not be a success in God's eyes. That's because God looks at the inside. He's not impressed with outward appearance; he looks at the heart (1 Sam. 16:7). So be careful how you measure success.

I remember talking with a friend who was sharing his disappointment over his inability to make a living doing music. He'd always dreamed about being a professional musician but had to settle instead for a job in the computer field. At the end of our conversation, my friend said something that caught my attention. "You know, when I really think about it, I guess I have every reason to be content. I have a good job, a great wife, a wonderful family, a thriving small group, and I get to play my horn regularly at church." What my friend is too humble to say, but what I can say for him, is that he is a success in God's eyes even though he never "made it" in music. He walks with Christ and is trying to grow in his relationship with the Lord. God is using him powerfully at church as he plays his horn and leads a small group. Something tells me he's more content now than he would have been had he become a professional musician. Those who strive to follow God instead of chasing worldly success find true contentment.

Follow-Up Questions for Group Discussion

1. As you were growing up, were you allowed to express your emotions freely, or were you taught to suppress them?
2. Why do you think it's awkward for people to encounter someone who's down or sad?
3. What should you do if you suspect someone is trying to get attention by creating his or her own emotional turmoil?
4. How do you feel when you're around someone who's constantly negative or critical? How does their attitude affect you?
5. What does it mean to dwell on God's truth? What are some ways to do that?

6. How can throwing yourself into worship help you manage your emotions?
7. How might it affect Sunday worship if your worship team were to practice gratitude on a regular basis?
8. How would it affect your church if congregation members were more content and filled with gratitude?

PERSONAL ACTION STEPS

1. Identify one thing you can do to be a more emotionally healthy person. Find someone to whom you can be accountable to follow through on that intention.
2. Commit to identify, every day for forty days, three things for which you are grateful.
3. Name one thing you can do for fun that can curb your tendency to take yourself too seriously.
4. Spend a significant block of time in solitude with God this week and talk to him about your pain, disappointment, and sadness.
5. Habakkuk 3:17–18 is written from the point of view of someone from an agrarian culture. Rewrite the passage from the perspective of a twenty-first-century worshiper.

CHAPTER 8

LEADING ARTISTS

TYLER IS SITTING IN HIS FIRST counseling session with Dr. Carlson. After months of prodding him, his wife and close friends finally succeeded in getting Tyler to see a therapist. Dr. Carlson came highly recommended. He and Tyler spent the first part of their session getting to know each other and discussing Dr. Carlson's approach as a Christian counselor. Now it's time to get down to business.

"Tell me, Tyler," Carlson begins, "why are you seeking counseling at this point in your life?"

Tyler shifts in his chair as he collects his thoughts. "I'm not exactly sure, Dr. Carlson. I . . . I think I'm having a midlife crisis."

"I see," replies the doctor. "You seem rather young to be grappling with midlife issues. How old are you?"

"I'm twenty-nine, sir." Tyler laughs. "I know it sounds silly, but I don't know what's going on with me." Carlson leans forward as Tyler continues. "I'm really discouraged about my job, and I'm unhappy with my life. I'm tired all the time, I have a hard time getting up in the morning, I have difficulty concentrating, I'm angry. My wife thinks I'm suffering from depression."

"Do you think you're depressed?" asks Dr. Carlson.

"I don't know," Tyler says, growing quiet.

"You mentioned your job. What is it that you do for a living?"

"I work for a church. I'm a worship leader."

"Tell me more about what's going on at church," Carlson probes.

"I just don't know if I'm cut out to be a leader," Tyler explains. "The musical part of my job is easy for me, but there's a lot more to this job than just doing music."

"Like what?"

"First of all," Tyler rolls his eyes, "there's meetings all the time, volunteers who need attention, services every week. Problems or conflicts come up all the time. I feel like I'm constantly putting out fires. There's no way I can keep up with all the demands. I feel like I'm always letting someone down, whether it's my team, my pastor, the church. I feel totally inadequate as a leader, like I'm a failure." Tyler takes a deep breath.

"I see. Has anything happened recently that has brought all these issues to the surface? Anything going on at work right now?"

"Well, yes," Tyler admits uneasily. "The pastor called me into his office last week to talk about a few things. It was a tough conversation. Apparently, some people in the congregation have been giving him an earful about the music. It's too loud, too edgy for some of the older folks. He also confronted me on dropping the ball on a project he assigned me over a month ago. He's really frustrated that I haven't added any new faces to the worship team this year. He questioned whether I'm using my time wisely. I love my pastor, Dr. Carlson, but it seems like I only hear from him when he's upset with me."

"Sorry to hear that, Tyler. Sounds like that meeting was pretty intense." Tyler nods in agreement. "What would you say is the hardest part of your job?"

Tyler doesn't hesitate. "It's the people."

"Go on," encourages Carlson. "What is it about the people that is so challenging?"

Again, Tyler struggles to put thoughts together. "I don't know. I suppose it has something to do with them all being artists. They can be temperamental, you know."

"Do you consider yourself an artist, Tyler?"

"Yes, but I barely know how to lead myself, let alone other artists. Sometimes I feel like I need someone to lead me."

The doctor ventures one last question. "Was there ever a time when you liked your job?"

"Oh yeah!" Tyler's eyes light up. "When I wasn't getting paid."

"What do you mean?"

"I loved leading worship when I first started doing it. Back then I was a volunteer at the church. I had time to work on the music. I used to write praise songs all the time. I love songwriting. I feel so alive when I'm working on a song. I miss those days. Sometimes I wonder if I should quit my job at the church, go back to my old job in computers, and lead worship on a volunteer basis. Volunteering is much more fun than leading."

Needing to bring their session to a close, Dr. Carlson starts to wrap up. "That sounds like a good place to stop for today. Let's pick up from there next week, Tyler. I want to thank you, though, for sharing. You've gotten us off to a good start. We have a lot to talk about over the next few months, but I think I can help you."

"Thanks." Tyler reaches to shake the doctor's hand. "I'm looking forward to next week. See you then." As he leaves the doctor's office, Tyler notices a bounce in his step. For the first time in months, he feels hopeful.

Questions for Group Discussion

1. Is it true that volunteering at church is more fun than leading?
2. What characterizes a great leader, in your opinion?
3. Can someone with an artistic temperament be a good leader? Why or why not?
4. How is it possible to meet all the demands and responsibilities of being a leader in the church?
5. If you were Tyler, what would you do to develop a better working relationship with the pastor?
6. What suggestions do you have for Tyler to help him manage his time?
7. How important do you think it might be for Tyler to write songs, like he used to? What changes do you think he needs to make in his job to allow him more time to write?
8. What words of advice do you have for someone starting out in church work?
9. If you're a leader, what do you struggle with most in your role?

Tension between Being a Leader and Being an Artist

An increasing number of church artists find themselves in positions of leadership, whether they aspired to that or not. But leading a ministry and doing artistic work are two different endeavors. The majority of books and seminars on leadership emerge from the business world and tend to reflect left brain cognition. They are generally data driven and present approaches to planning, strategizing, and problem solving that are ordered, logical, and linear. Artists tend to be more right-brained. We are instinctive, creative, and nonlinear. We generate innovative ideas and creative solutions. The successful leader championed by the business world is usually a confident, driven, and dynamic extrovert. But many artists are introverts who feel like a fish out of water doing non-artistic things. I've heard numerous artists confess that they feel much more comfortable standing onstage with a guitar in their hands or sitting behind a soundboard than leading meetings. Many never saw themselves as leaders until they were thrust into the role. As a result, they feel torn between their calling as an artist and the demands of leadership.

Can you relate to any of this? Do you ever feel a tension between the artist in you and the leader in you? Do you ever doubt your calling? Do you ever wonder if you're really in the right place or whether you're doing what God really wants you to do? Do you ever feel restless? Do you ever find yourself fantasizing about that dream job?

Artists who step into church leadership often do so at the risk of stifling their artistic side. The administrative demands can prevent us from practicing or creating to the extent we used to. Some arts leaders are so preoccupied with developing and empowering other artists that their own giftedness falls by the wayside. For many of us, the coming together of our art and our faith has been a deeply personal, spiritual experience. According to Scripture, we are "God's handiwork, created in Christ Jesus to do good works, which God prepared in advance for us to do" (Eph. 2:10). Some of those good works that artists are destined to do involve our craft. Being denied an artistic outlet because of excessive leadership demands can be frustrating.

For a long time I resented my leadership responsibilities because they took me away from doing music, especially songwriting. I reached a crisis point and decided that something needed to change. I was exhausted from trying to be an artist and a leader. Convinced that I wasn't adequately fulfilling either role, I felt discouraged and frustrated. I realized I needed to choose between leadership and music. Either throw myself into leading and forget about music or step down from leadership to focus on music. There's no way I could do both. At least that's what I thought.

Not the Answer I Was Looking For

Driven by my self-imposed pressure to choose, I spent several days searching Scripture, praying, journaling. I noticed that when Jesus sent the disciples out on their first missionary assignment, he "gave them authority to drive out impure spirits and to heal every disease and sickness" (Matt. 10:1). Jesus not only clarified what he wanted them to do but empowered them to do it. I asked the Lord to do the same thing for me—make my calling clear. "Lord, settle this issue once and for all," I prayed. "What are you authorizing and empowering me to do? Do you want me to write songs or lead a worship ministry?"

An answer eventually came, but it was not the answer I was hoping for. I sensed the Lord calling me to do both—write music and lead a community of artists. Of course, I did not give in easily. I reminded the Lord that I couldn't see how anyone could be a productive leader and flourish as an artist. God seemed to simply reply, "I'll show you how. I'll help you figure this out. Trust me."

In the ensuing years, God has taught me much about navigating the tricky terrain between artistry and leadership. Today I have the privilege of mentoring young men and women whom God has called to do both. The first step for those of us in this position is to stop viewing it as an either-or proposition; it is instead a both-and situation. The only way to resolve the tension between being an artist and being a leader is to embrace God's invitation to do both.

Don't Let Your Talent Fall by the Wayside

Paul admonished young Timothy never to neglect his gift (1 Tim. 4:14). By the same token, I urge all worship-and-the-arts leaders not to neglect their gifts. Don't stop being an artist now that you're a leader. It doesn't matter whether you're a virtuoso performer or you merely dabble in the arts. Embrace the part of you that appreciates artistry and loves to do artistic things.

If you're an instrumentalist, pick up your instrument and play. Make it a point to practice and keep your chops in shape. Learn those jazz riffs or that classical piece you've always wanted to play. If you sing, keep your voice in shape so you can still lead worship from time to time. Learn a song that you'll never use in church, just for the fun of it. If you write, write. Work on that short story or song or novel you've always wanted to write. If you're a poet, invite a few friends over for an informal reading of your poems. If you're in media or the technical arts, look for opportunities to exercise those talents, even if it's on a small scale or just for family and friends. Make sure your talent doesn't get lost now that you're in leadership. Look for outlets for your artistic gifts.

You will undoubtedly have to take initiative so that your

artistic gifts don't fall by the wayside. Don't expect someone else to do this for you. You need to be proactive in these matters. You may also need to get creative with your solutions. When all this came to a head for me, I couldn't see a way forward until I gave myself permission to think outside the box. That's when I came up with the idea of building writing breaks into my schedule. I asked my supervisor if I could work at home a couple of days a month. It was unusual at that time and in that setting for a staff member to work at home. But she graciously allowed me to pull out of meetings once a month to arrange and write music. That radical move protected my musical abilities from getting lost in the avalanche of my administrative duties. It also helped me to be more productive in my leadership role at the church.

Step into Leadership

If you lead a ministry in the worship arts, I also encourage you to throw yourself into leadership. Learn all you can about what it takes to be an effective leader so you can be the best leader you can be. Don't worry if you don't fit the leader stereotype emulated by the business world. God hasn't called you to lead a business. He's called you to lead a community of artists. I've come to the conclusion that the best person to lead artists is another artist. Don't shrink back, waiting for someone to empower or validate you. If you've been called to lead a ministry, Jesus has given you authority to lead. So take ownership. Take initiative. "God has not given us a spirit of timidity, but of power and love and discipline" (2 Tim. 1:7 NASB). Don't hold back. Don't be a passive leader. Be as assertive as you're comfortable being. Stepping into leadership means you accept that you are a spiritual leader whose mission is to serve God by serving his people.

EMBRACE SPIRITUAL LEADERSHIP

If you lead a church ministry, you are a spiritual leader. At first I was intimidated by the thought of leading others spiritually, especially those in my ministry who were older in years or in the faith. Yet I quickly realized that the people I led viewed me as their pastor or shepherd, just by virtue of my position. Though I stepped into spiritual leadership with fear and trepidation, embracing my role made me understand that I wasn't merely building a vibrant arts program or worship ministry. My goal was to build a healthy community of artists.

To achieve that kind of community, I needed to accept the mantle of spiritual leadership. Peter instructs leaders, "Be shepherds of God's flock that is under your care" (1 Peter 5:2). Since I am the spiritual leader of my team, it is my job to care for the souls of the artists God brings my way. Ministry, after all, is people. God invites you and me to invest in the lives of others. It would be a shame to get to the end of our lives and discover that all we had to show for our hard work was a few worship recordings. What about the people? Will our artists be better off spiritually because they served under our leadership? Don't just gather artists and fail to build into them.

The writer of Proverbs assumes that shepherds know the condition of their flocks and give "careful attention" to those under their charge (Prov. 27:23). Faithful shepherds make the effort to spend time with their people to get to know them. They take initiative by scheduling lunch or coffee. They hang out with their team. It takes a lot of commitment to be involved in worship ministry. Volunteers sacrifice a great deal and give a lot of their time to rehearse, prepare, and put on services. I've observed that team members are more apt to remain loyal and committed to ministry over the long haul if they feel cared for and have some semblance of relationship with their leader. Effective spiritual leaders invest time and energy into building relationships with their people.

EMBRACE SERVANT LEADERSHIP

Jesus served those he led and instructs us to follow his example (Mark 10:45; John 13:14). Instead of serving his own selfish ambition and agenda, the Son of God served the Father by serving people. Jesus' leadership style can prove challenging for artists. We're encouraged to assert our talents and sell ourselves to get ahead. Servant leadership is not about getting ahead; it's about taking a back seat when necessary to allow the gifts of others to be elevated.

Jesus' style of leadership revolutionized my approach to ministry. I realized that my goal as a leader is to set up other people for meaningful ministry opportunities. I will contend till the day I die that there is no greater thrill in life than to be used of God. In my book, nothing beats knowing that God has used me and my humble talents to impact another life. When my younger son was a teenager, he used to run sound and lights for the children's program at our church. I remember driving home with him after the service one night, and I asked him how the kids' program went. He proudly replied, "It went well. I really feel God used me this weekend." Embracing servant leadership allows us to see others, possibly even our own children, experience the joy and fulfillment of God's using their talents for his glory.

In 1 Thessalonians 2, the apostle Paul offers further guidelines, based on traditional mother-father roles, on what it means to be a servant leader. Let's consider what this passage teaches us about leading artists.

Be Gentle and Sensitive

Paul reminds the Thessalonians that he was gentle with them, like a mother caring for her little children (1 Thess. 2:7). We too need to be gentle and sensitive with the artists we lead. I've heard people dismiss the suggestion that they be gentler because they're "not wired that way." That may be true, but it should never be used as an excuse for a lack of sensitivity. Scripture commands us to be tenderhearted toward each other, even if we're not wired that way (Prov. 25:11; Col. 3:12–13; Eph. 4:32). Gentleness is also one of the fruits of the Spirit (Gal. 5:22–23). Jesus said, "Blessed are the gentle, for they shall inherit the earth" (Matt. 5:5 NASB). Jesus didn't just preach gentleness, he practiced it.

I once spent several weeks reading the gospels, trying to discover Jesus' secret for dealing with people. What was it about Jesus that made Mary drop what she was doing, risk the disapproval of her sister, and sit at his feet? What was it about Jesus that compelled a despised tax collector and a forsaken prostitute to leave their former lives and follow him? What was it about Jesus that comforted Jairus and assured him that his sick daughter was going to be all right? I believe it was more than Jesus' words. I think it was the way he looked at people, something about his eyes. I'm convinced that Jesus looks at human beings with such compassion that merely catching his eye can be a holy moment that draws us deeper into loving communion with him.

Proverbs states that "bright eyes gladden the heart" (15:30 NASB). People can tell how you feel about them simply by how you look at them, or whether you look at them at all. The writer of Proverbs notes that "when a king's face brightens, it means life; his favor is like a rain cloud in spring" (16:15). Leaders can set the tone for a meeting or conversation without saying a word, because their subordinates are always reading their faces, trying to gauge how the boss is responding.

My fellow leaders, whether you're aware of it or not, how you feel about those you lead registers on your face. They can see it in your eyes. If those under you see your face light up when you see them, they will feel accepted. They will be drawn to you because the look of love and acceptance in your eyes gives them life. Try it and see if it works. Try to communicate gentle compassion without words, with just your face or your eyes. Try looking at your spouse, your kids, coworkers, teammates with facial expressions that communicate approval and acceptance.

Another way to show sensitivity to the people in your life is to listen to their feelings. Invite them to talk about what's going on in their lives. Let them share their stories. Don't offer advice without completely listening. Be quick to hear and slow to speak (James 1:19). Show those artists you lead that you care about them as people by listening to what's on their hearts and minds.

Treating someone gently and with sensitivity doesn't mean we fail to be firm when the situation calls for it. Leaders need to discern when to be tender and when to be firm. First Thessalonians 5:14 tells us to "admonish the unruly, encourage the fainthearted" (NASB). Unfortunately,

I sometimes get that turned around. I encourage someone who's being stubborn and unruly, and I'm hard on someone who's weak and fainthearted, someone who needs me to be tender. I've made that mistake with my wife, my kids, and the artists I work with. Proverbs 25:11 says, "A word fitly spoken is like apples of gold in settings of silver" (NKJV). It takes discernment and a sensitivity to the Holy Spirit to have the right words at the right time, to know what to say and what not to say, but it's essential if you want to become a more sensitive leader. I find myself praying often, sometimes in the middle of a conversation, *Lord, do you want me to be gentle with this person or firm?*

Love Them

Paul writes to the Thessalonians, "Because we loved you so much, we were delighted to share with you not only the gospel of God but our lives as well" (1 Thess. 2:8). Paul was a leader who not only loved the church but loved the people in the church. The congregation at Thessalonica had become near and dear to his heart. Paul and his fellow leaders demonstrated love by giving of themselves to others.

What does it look like for you to love on your artists? One way to show love to creative types is to ask them what project they're working on. Ask them to play you that new song they're slaving over or that new poem they're working on or that painting they're excited about. Take a genuine interest in your artists. Find out what they do for a living, what they do for fun, where they like to vacation. Know the names of their spouses, even their children if possible. Show your artists that you cherish them, that you appreciate them not only for their talent but for who they are as a brother or sister in Christ.

Exhort Them

Having extoled the virtues of gentleness, sensitivity, and love, Paul now takes on a more fatherly tone and aggressively exhorts the believers at Thessalonica. To exhort means to urge someone toward a goal or an accomplishment (1 Thess. 2:11–12). Like Paul, we need to urge our artists to achieve all they can for the glory of God, to fulfill their calling, to flourish in their giftedness. Keep calling your artists to the level of excellence they're capable of achieving. Those who are exceptionally talented appreciate being pushed.

Many of us have sat under the direction of dynamic choir directors, producers, or leaders who were demanding in ways that brought out the best in us. They set the bar high and convinced us we could attain more than we thought we could. There's nothing wrong with demanding the best of artists, especially in a safe environment where they feel loved and cherished. It's okay to demand that artists be the best they can be, not for their own vain glory (or ours) but for the glory of God. Urge team members to live up to their potential as artists.

Encourage Them

Paul went out of his way to encourage his flock (1 Thess. 2:11–12). Artists thrive on encouragement, so offer it liberally; comfort them with encouraging words when they need it. Don't assume your artists know that something they did was good or exceptional. Even if they do, it's still nice to hear it. "Do not withhold good from those to whom it is due" (Prov. 3:27). Let team members know, verbally or in writing, how you feel about their work.

Moses called on a number of artists to help him build the tabernacle. When the project was completed, "Moses inspected the work and saw that they had done it just as the Lord had commanded. So Moses blessed them" (Ex. 39:43). Notice that Moses didn't send a representative. He met personally with the builders and artists and examined their work. Then he blessed them. He encouraged them. He honored them and celebrated the contribution they had made. Encouragement goes a long way with artists.

Words of comfort and encouragement are even more appreciated when someone fails. Many artists suffer from self-doubt and discouragement when they fail. If a teammate's efforts fall short, be sure to check in and make sure he or she is okay. Assure discouraged team members that you still believe in them and in their abilities. Help your artists put their failures into perspective.

Implore Them

Last, Paul also made a point of imploring those under his leadership (1 Thess. 2:11 NASB). To implore means to beseech, challenge, or charge. Paul implored his people to "live lives worthy of God" (1 Thess. 2:12). We too need to implore our artists to live lives of godly integrity, to glorify God with the way they live, not just the way they play or sing. Spiritual leaders must always be willing to confront sin in ourselves as well as in those we lead. Confronting a brother or sister about an observable pattern of sin should always be done with humility, compassion, and love. Always confront sin with the goal of restoring the wayward individual to a right relationship with God and the church (Gal. 6:1). If you implore your team members to live lives worthy of their calling as artists in the church, you will have served them well.

Why Is Ministry So Hard?

One of the reasons I assumed that I had to choose between being an artist and being a leader was because I was frustrated trying to do both. I wanted life (and ministry) to be easy—no obstacles or conflicts, please. So when it wasn't easy, I thought I was doing something wrong or was slotted in the wrong role or maybe was at the wrong church. I'll be the first to confess that I have an unhealthy need for a hassle-free life.

I want everything to be easy and things to run smoothly. When ministry is difficult, I find myself thinking (actually whining), *Come on, Lord, I work hard. Give me a break. Does everything always have to be so hard?* Somehow I think I deserve life to be easy. That's not only prideful, it's unrealistic. In *Letters to a Young Poet*, Rainer Maria Rilke writes, "People have, with the help of so many conventions, resolved everything the easy way, on the easiest side of easy. But it is clear that we must embrace struggle. Every living thing conforms to it. Everything in nature grows and struggles in its own way, establishing its own identity, insisting on it at all cost, against all resistance. We can be sure of very little, but the need to court struggle is surety that will not leave us. It is good to be lonely, for being alone is not easy. The fact that something is difficult must be one more reason to do it."[49]

If ministry doesn't go smoothly, that doesn't mean God isn't in it. If a task isn't easy, that doesn't mean we shouldn't be doing it.

Ask Moses if being a leader was ever difficult. Ask Nehemiah if rebuilding Jerusalem's wall was challenging. Ask Job if life ever got hard. Ask Jeremiah if doing God's will always went smoothly. Ask Paul if ministry ever got dangerous. The easy life is simply unrealistic, and it's not the life Jesus is calling us to live. Why did Paul tell us not to lose heart and give up doing good (Gal. 6:9) if the Christian life is supposed to be easy?

Jesus never promised that ministry would be problem free. When he commissioned his disciples for ministry, he warned them that he was throwing them to the wolves (Matt. 10:16). He told them to expect conflict so severe that they'd be handed over to the local authorities and flogged (v. 17). He predicted that friends and family would turn against them and that people would hate them (vv. 21–22). They'd be on the run, getting kicked out of one town and moving on to the next (v. 23). Jesus was brutally honest about the challenges of doing ministry.

Like the first band of disciples, we too need to go into church work with our eyes wide open and face the reality that ministry can be difficult. Whether you're part of a large church or in a smaller setting, every facet of worship ministry—song selection, raising up volunteers, rehearsals, services, technical matters—is fraught with difficulty and comes with its own pressure.

Paul was reporting from the front lines of ministry when he spoke of being hard pressed on every side, perplexed, persecuted, and struck down (2 Cor. 4:8–9). Paul endured a lot more hardship in ministry than I'll probably ever see. His life was often in danger, he was attacked and beaten, he was shipwrecked and almost lost at sea. I have never suffered physical abuse doing church work. I've had it easy compared with Paul. Yet I can still relate to the adversity Paul is describing. I can relate to feeling hard pressed on every side, stressed out and pressured by the demands of ministry. I have been perplexed by issues and problems I had no solutions for. I have even felt persecuted by congregation members who didn't like a decision I made or got upset with me about something that occurred in a service. While I can't say I've ever been literally struck down like Paul, I have felt beaten down by ministry and beaten up by church people. There were times I wanted to quit because I was so discouraged. While Paul's ministry was far more dangerous than mine, what he's depicting in this passage does not feel foreign to my experience as a leader in the church.

Words of Encouragement from Jesus

After Jesus warned the disciples of the dangers awaiting them, he sent them out on their short-term mission trip with words of encouragement (Matt. 10:26–31). Three times during this brief discourse, he tells them not to be afraid. What fears or concerns do you have as a leader right now? Are you afraid of changes happening in your ministry these days? Are you afraid of failing? Are you afraid that you won't be a good leader? Are you afraid that you'll never be fulfilled as an artist-leader? Jesus tells us not to fear because he is with us. My fellow leaders, the Lord will not leave you or forsake you (Deut. 31:8; Josh. 1:5; Heb. 13:5).

Jesus loves us too much to abandon us and let us fend for ourselves. He reminded the disciples of their great worth in the eyes of God the Father: "Are not two sparrows sold for a penny? Yet not one of them will fall to the ground outside your Father's care. And even the very hairs of your head are all numbered. So don't be afraid; you are worth more than many sparrows" (Matt. 10:29–31). You are precious to the Lord, my friend. He knows you intimately, down to the last hair on your head. He knows what you're feeling. He knows your discouragement; he sees your weariness. He's aware of how hard ministry is and all the challenges facing you. He knows the tensions you live with every day. Know that God cares for you and is there for you in the midst of all your trials and travails.

When Paul tells Christians to "be steadfast, immovable, always abounding in the work of the Lord" (1 Cor. 15:58 NASB), he addresses us as his "dear brothers and sisters" (NIV). You are not just another faceless worker on the Christian assembly line of disciple makers. You are not merely another unknown soldier in God's army. You are not a forgotten worker in the kingdom of God. You are God's beloved child. You are known and cherished by the one who created you, gifted you, and called you into ministry and into leadership. Go forth, therefore, in the strong name of Jesus, who will never leave you or forsake you because he loves you more than you'll ever know.

Follow-Up Questions for Group Discussion

1. Have you experienced any tension between being an artist and being a leader? What has that been like for you?
2. What can you do to make sure that your artistic talent doesn't get lost amid all the duties and demands of leadership?
3. Can you remember your favorite choir director or drama director or some leader who inspired you to go farther with your talent? What was it about this leader that inspired you so much?
4. What, in your opinion, characterizes an effective spiritual leader?
5. What are some examples of things leaders can do to help their artists grow spiritually?
6. Which of the five keys for nurturing artists (being sensitive, loving them, exhorting them, encouraging them, imploring them) do you think is most important and why?
7. What are some of the biggest challenges facing you as a ministry leader these days?
8. If you're a leader, what would you like to say at this time to those you lead?
9. If you're under someone's leadership, is there anything you'd like to say to your leader?

PERSONAL ACTION STEPS

1. Devise a plan to ensure that your artistic talent doesn't fall by the wayside. Be sure to think outside the box if necessary.
2. Identify the areas of your ministry where you need to exert more leadership.
3. Think about what it means for you to invest in the spiritual lives of your artists. What is the next action step for you in that regard?
4. List the names of three people in your ministry with whom you'd like to meet over a meal or coffee to get to know them better.
5. Ask the Lord if there's someone in your ministry he wants you to disciple. Set up a meeting with that person to talk about the possibility of getting together regularly for one-on-one discipleship.
6. Of the five keys for nurturing artists (being sensitive, loving them, exhorting them, encouraging them, imploring them), choose the one you need to focus on most this next year.

CHAPTER 9

THE ARTIST AND SIN

MATT WAS THE MOST TALENTED AND successful worship leader that Oakville Community Church had ever had. Thanks to Matt, Oakville had the largest worship ministry in the area. The church had even become known more for its music than for anything else. Under Matt's leadership, the worship team produced two live recordings that were highly successful, circulated widely outside the church, and gained national recognition. Churches across the country were singing songs written by the team at Oakville. Matt's notoriety began to grow. He received more invitations to speak at worship conferences than he could accept. He became widely known as a dynamic worship leader, songwriter, and visionary. In his five short years at Oakville, Matt had attained success, status, and popularity.

Just when he was at the apex of his ministry career, Matt's world came crashing down. The news broke that he was having an affair with one of the women in his ministry. It had started out innocently. Veronica was an excellent singer, and she and Matt began spending a lot of time together rehearsing. They soon realized there was a spark between them, and they fanned the flames of a passionate relationship. Veronica had never met anyone as encouraging and sensitive as Matt. She felt she had finally found her soul mate. Her husband wasn't very supportive of her as a person or as a singer, and she began to look for, and even create, opportunities to spend time with Matt.

Matt's marriage had been slowly deteriorating as he threw himself into his job and his wife threw herself into raising three toddlers. After meeting Veronica, Matt felt that she was everything he had ever wanted, and he was convinced that he had married the wrong person. His relationship with Veronica was so much easier than his relationship with his wife. They got along so much better, he thought.

Matt daydreamed and fantasized about Veronica a lot and couldn't wait to see her at rehearsal. They often rehearsed alone, just the two of them. When rehearsal spilled over into the noon hour, it gave them an excuse to have lunch together. Matt began working late at church, rehearsing with Veronica. He knew the relationship was wrong. He kept telling himself it had to end, but when he was with her, the physical and emotional attraction was so strong that he couldn't bring himself to end it. He knew he was jeopardizing his marriage and his career, but he was getting things from Veronica that he wasn't getting at home. A fellow staff member confronted Matt about how much time he was spending with Veronica, but Matt got defensive and denied anything was going on. Covering up the affair was exhausting, but it was the only way to keep seeing Veronica and still keep his job. Veronica also knew deep inside that this relationship was not right, but the pull was too strong for her too. She knew she was putting her marriage at risk, but only if people found out. She and Matt talked about running away together and starting over with a clean slate.

The affair continued for months. Their relationship got more and more involved. Finally, Matt's wife, and subsequently Veronica's husband, found out. The whole church found out too. Matt confessed to the entire congregation about the affair. He was humiliated and broken. He admitted the deception. He even confessed to other dark areas of his life, such as his addiction to pornography. That caught everybody by surprise.

Matt was asked to resign his position immediately and was advised to seek counseling. The church split into factions, and people argued over how the whole thing was handled. Some even left the church. There were those who blamed the church because they felt Matt was overworked, so the church, in their minds, was the cause of the affair. Some thought Matt should be retained and that the church should work with him and love him back into fellowship. Others thought he should be banned from ministry for good. Still others resented Veronica and thought she should have been asked to leave instead of Matt. It was quite a mess.

Matt's wife divorced him and won custody of their children. He lost his job, his ministry, his wife, his family, and his reputation. He moved away, was never heard from again, and never saw Veronica again. And he never worked at a church again.

Veronica and her husband also divorced. She tried to stay at the church, but the shame she felt made it too difficult. She couldn't bear having to face all those people at church every week, especially Matt's wife and kids. She thought of running away with Matt. She almost did, but their relationship had started to sour after everything hit the fan. Anger and resentment had begun to take its toll. The spark that had once ignited between Matt and Veronica had turned into a devastating fire that ravaged both their lives. Neither was ever the same.

Questions for Group Discussion

1. What bad decisions did Matt make that contributed to his fall?
2. What bad decisions did Veronica make?
3. What caused this affair? What factors enabled it to happen?
4. What were the consequences of the affair?
5. How could the affair have been avoided?
6. Would you feel comfortable confronting someone if you saw him or her involved with sin? Why or why not?
7. Do you agree with how the church handled this situation? If not, how should the church have handled it?
8. How prevalent do you think the problem of pornography is today among Christians?

Susceptibility to Sin

If this scenario sounds familiar to you, it's because the story is all too common. You may have heard of, witnessed, or even been involved in an extramarital affair that ruined lives and tore apart your church. Why does this sort of thing happen as often as it does? What causes a fall like this? And how do you know that what happened to Matt and Veronica won't happen to you?

I know I'm going out on a limb when I say this, but I believe that those of us with artistic temperaments are more susceptible to sin than any other group of people. It seems sin is always crouching at our door (Gen. 4:7). The gifts and talents of the artistic temperament often put us in the thick of God's activities. Many of us are on the front lines of ministry. We're highly visible because we're on the platform regularly. We are prime targets for the Evil One, who would love nothing more than for us to fall and disgrace the cause of Christ. Like Matt in our opening scenario, many of us spend a great deal of time rehearsing and performing with members of the opposite sex. Satan often tries to use intimate contact like that to break up marriages and create scandal. Remember, the devil always prowls about like a roaring lion, looking to devour any artists he can (1 Peter 5:8).

The artistic temperament makes us easy victims for "the lust of the flesh, the lust of the eyes, and the pride of life" (1 John 2:16). Many of us are in touch with our feelings. When lustful desires are combined with highly charged emotions, it's like putting gasoline on a fire. Many of us are also very aware of our senses. We like to be stimulated, especially visually, which opens us up to all sorts of sinful desires. We are passionate people, so we need to make sure that our passions don't get out of control. Because we're often in the spotlight, we end up dealing with all sorts of pride and arrogance issues.

We can also be very self-centered, even preoccupied with ourselves, resulting in selfish motives. Our sensitivity causes us to be hurt more easily and more often. I think this is why so many artists carry around a great deal of anger, bitterness, and resentment. As we discussed earlier, our introspection also tends to make us more negative and critical.

We also have vivid imaginations. It's the nature of creativity to let your mind drift and be free, but a renegade imagination can also lead to sin. Most of us would be embarrassed if people saw our thoughts flashed on a movie screen. Jesus made a connection between our thoughts and our behavior (Matt. 5:27–28). An X-rated fantasy life does not produce G-rated behavior. Even if we never do a fraction of the things we fantasize about, we still do untold damage to our souls by entertaining ungodly thoughts.

Christian artists who struggle with obsessive, compulsive, and escapist tendencies sometimes turn to alcohol, drugs, or pornography to avoid dealing with the pain in their lives. Sadly, instead of getting help, they hide their secret addiction and lead double lives, projecting an image of piety at church but living quite differently when alone.

So there you have it. We are people who are more susceptible to lust of the flesh, lust of the eyes, pride, arrogance, selfish motives, anger, bitterness, resentment, a negative and critical spirit, impure thoughts, compulsive and addictive behavior, and hypocrisy and duplicity. Not a great recipe for godly living! Those of us with artistic temperaments have an uphill battle when it comes to living holy lives.

The Seriousness of Sin

Sin is a serious matter; it's what separates us from God. It's why Jesus came to die on the cross. It's why our world is in such a mess. It's why there's a heaven and a hell. We cannot be cavalier about sin. There are no special exemptions just because you're a successful artist. Second Timothy 2:21 says that if we cleanse ourselves from sin, we will be "instruments for special purposes, made holy, useful to the Master and prepared to do any good work." You can't make allowances for sin in your life and expect God to use you to your fullest. Make no mistake about it. Sin grieves the Holy Spirit and quenches the power of God in our lives.

We deceive ourselves if we think we can live in sin and get by on talent alone. It's a deadly deception because at first it might seem true. You can go far on talent alone. I've known a few artists who were living a double life and using their talents with seeming success, until their secret life caught up to them. You can go far, but you can't go long. Eventually "your sin will find you out" (Num. 32:23). Besides, it is much more fulfilling to have God work through you than around you. In your life right now, is there any sin that could keep God from using you to your full potential?

When we take sin lightly, we underestimate the value of a clear conscience (1 Tim. 1:5, 19; 3:9). Having a clear conscience doesn't mean we're perfect. It means we've confessed all known sin, we've made amends with those we've offended, and we're striving to live in obedience to Christ. The person who has a clear conscience is free from guilt and shame because they're quick to repent and make amends. In your life right now, is there any sin that is keeping you from having a clear conscience?

Paul tried to avoid sin so as not to discredit his ministry (2 Cor. 6:3). If you are an up-front, highly visible person at your church, as many artists are, you have a responsibility to deal with the sin in your life so as to uphold the witness of your church and protect God's reputation. Sometimes during an audition, I'll run across a musician who's living with a boyfriend or girlfriend. When I suggest that living together outside of marriage is not appropriate behavior for the artists in our church, he or she responds with indignation. They can't understand why I would deprive our congregation of their great talent because of "one little sin."

We should not tolerate any willful disobedience in our lives. So let's state clearly that it is wrong to be living with your boyfriend or girlfriend outside of marriage. It is wrong to flirt with immorality. It is also wrong to gossip and slander. No matter how talented you are, you are not above

God's laws, and you need to take responsibility for sin in your life. If you don't, it bears repeating: your sin will find you out, and so will everyone else.

I realize that I'm addressing people with perfectionistic tendencies, so I need to emphasize that I'm not talking about being perfect. I'm stating that the general direction of our lives should reflect a sincere effort to obey the Lord's commands.

A Word to Those Battling Addictions

My dear artistic friend, if you're involved right now in some secret sin or addiction, please see a Christian therapist, counselor, or pastor. According to Cornelius Plantinga, "An addict stands a chance of recovery only if he is finally willing to tell himself the truth. The only way out of the addict's plight is through it. He has to face it, deal with it, confess it. With the firm and caring support of people important to him, he has to rip his way through all the tissues of denial and self-deception that have 'protected his supply.' The addict has to take a hard step, the first of the famous twelve steps. Paradoxically, he must help himself by admitting that he is helpless. He must perform the courageous, difficult, and highly responsible act of acknowledging the hopelessness and wholesale unmanageability of his life."[50]

Don't live in denial about your addiction. Please get the help you need before it's too late.

Accountable Relationships

In my experience helping artists deal with sin, I've observed that we artistic types are weak in two areas: setting up accountable relationships and doing spiritual battle. Being accountable to someone is the first step in addressing sin in our lives. James 5:16 says, "Confess your sins to each other and pray for each other so that you may be healed." Having to confess sin to an accountability partner can help us avoid that behavior in the future. Knowing we'll have to confess it makes us less apt to do it. Whether you're accountable to one person or a group of people, accountability is a must in the spiritual life.

Some of us dismiss accountability, believing we can handle life on our own. That is such a lie. Ignoring our need for accountable relationships leaves us vulnerable to temptation and gives Satan an open invitation to knock us off. Some of us who are more introverted might feel threatened by the thought of sharing our sins and temptations with others. We're afraid of what people might think of us when they find out we struggle in certain areas. I've heard artists express fear of getting kicked off the team if they were honest about their sin, so they try to hide it from others. Meanwhile their dark side grows more impervious to the light of Christ. They keep giving in to temptation. Addiction grows more intense. They cross lines and act out in ways they never dreamed possible. Hiding our sin instead of remaining accountable to a small group of trusted friends can prove to be a deadly trap.

Every time I've spoken with those who have been disqualified from ministry because of sin, they're always deeply sorry that they didn't call out sooner for help and support. It's ironic that they were so afraid to be transparent, because when they fell, their sins were made public and they were ashamed and embarrassed. They were too proud, too afraid, too stubborn, and they paid a high price. Paul tells us to make whatever changes we need to make to avoid being disqualified from ministry (1 Cor. 9:27). Establishing accountability should be high on your list of things to do, especially if you're involved in worship ministry in any way.

The Bible says, "As iron sharpens iron, so one person sharpens another" (Prov. 27:17). That's the beauty of accountable relationships. We can help each other and keep each other sharp. As a young man, I was in an accountability group with some guys who wanted to help each other deal with lust. We were brutally honest with each other, called each other when we needed help, and prayed regularly for each other. Part of what kept me from doing something stupid was knowing that I had guys in my life who were going to ask me, "How are you doing with lust this week?"

To this day I still have people in my life for accountability because the potential to fall lies in all of us and I don't want to fall. Don't be deceived and think you can make it on your own; we all need accountability. "If you think you are standing firm," writes Paul, "be careful that you don't fall!" (1 Cor. 10:12). Christians stronger than you and I have fallen simply because they thought they were above the need for accountability. Don't let this happen to you. Find someone or a group of people to whom you can be accountable.[51]

Learn How to Do Spiritual Battle

In addition to accountability, we need to learn how to engage in spiritual battle so we can stand up to the temptations that wage war against our souls (1 Peter 2:11). Spiritual warfare begins in our minds, which is why Paul instructs us to renew our minds (Rom. 12:2). When I became a Christian, I was plagued with a thought life that put me in competition with Paul for the title chief of sinners (1 Tim. 1:16). I didn't do most of the things I thought about, but I knew that the fantasies I regularly entertained were not pleasing to God. For me, step one in the Holy Spirit's work of renewing my mind called for me to stop indulging in sinful fantasies. If you want to live a holy life, if you want to change negative patterns of behavior, begin changing how you think. If you want to overcome temptation or break free from the bondage of sin, start establishing new thought patterns. Learn to think differently.

Ephesians 6:12 says that "our struggle is not against flesh and blood, but against the rulers, against the authorities, against the powers of this dark world and against the spiritual forces of evil in the heavenly realms." The word struggle is significant. The King James Version uses the word wrestle. Both words underscore the need for us to be proactive when it comes to sin. We need to resist temptation instead of letting ourselves be pulled along by it. Doing spiritual battle is serious business. It's warfare! We are instructed to wear armor (Eph. 6:11, 13). We are told to gird our minds for action (1 Peter 1:13). Yet many of us go through our day oblivious to and unprepared for the spiritual battles ahead of us.

James 4:7 tells us, "Resist the devil, and he will flee from you." But how many of us do that? How many of us know how to resist Satan? Most of us have never been taught how to stand up to the sinful thoughts that pop into our minds every day. Scripture assures us that the weapons at our disposal for battling temptation are powerful enough to destroy strongholds (2 Cor. 10:4), but we have to know how to use them. We must learn how to do spiritual battle. Let's turn to Matthew 4:1–11 and observe how Jesus did spiritual battle.

Jesus in Spiritual Battle

Matthew indicates that the Holy Spirit led Jesus into the wilderness to be tempted by the devil (Matt. 4:1). Satan's first temptation appealed to Jesus' physical needs (fig. 1). Jesus had been fasting for forty days and forty nights. He was

FIG. 1
Jesus Doing Spiritual Battle
Matthew 4:1–11
If you are the Son of God, command that these stones become bread.
It is written, "Man shall not live on bread alone, but on every word that proceeds out of the mouth of God."
If you are the Son of God throw Yourself down; for it is written, "He will give His angels charge concerning You; and on their hands they will bear You up, lest You strike Your foot against a stone."
On the other hand, it is written, "You shall not tempt the Lord your God."
All these things will I give You, if You fall down and worship me.
Be gone, Satan! For it is written, "You shall worship the Lord your God, and serve Him only."

hungry. Satan said, in effect, "Come on, Jesus. You've been working so hard. You deserve a break today. Turn these stones into bread." Satan will always try to get us to meet our needs apart from God. Jesus didn't entertain the notion Satan put into his head, as we sometimes do. He didn't fantasize about eating a full-course meal at Satan's table. Jesus quickly answered by quoting Scripture (Matt. 4:4).

Satan knows Scripture too, and he twisted it around to tempt Jesus a second time. He took the Son of God to the pinnacle of the temple and commanded him to throw himself down. This would have created a huge spectacle, with a host of angels coming to Jesus' rescue. Talk about making an entrance! What a spectacular scene that would have made. Satan wanted Jesus to use his supernatural power for personal gain. That's the same temptation artists face—using our talents and abilities to glorify ourselves. Jesus again didn't give it a second thought but instead responded to Satan's lies with the truth of Scripture (Matt. 4:7).

Satan didn't give up. His next temptation appeals to our human tendency to desire fame, fortune, and power. He took Jesus to the top of a mountain, showed him the kingdoms of the world, and said, "I will give you all this if you worship me." The Evil One offered Jesus what he tries to offer us artists: fame and fortune if we compromise our beliefs, our morals, our convictions. Jesus said, "Away from me, Satan!" and renounced the sin of idolatry, once more quoting Scripture (Matt. 4:10).

Notice three things about how Jesus handled temptation: (1) he countered quickly, (2) he countered with truth, and (3) he renounced sin. Let's unpack each of these.

I. COUNTER QUICKLY

Jesus opposed Satan's attack immediately. He didn't let himself fantasize about the thoughts Satan put in his mind, which is what we often do. As I stated earlier, we artists have very fertile imaginations, and we have no business entertaining the ungodly thoughts that come our way. Sin starts in the mind. Instead of letting sinful thoughts linger in our minds, we are to "resist the devil" (James 4:7). I realize that's not always easy, for we live in a culture that encourages us to indulge our appetites. C. S. Lewis describes how our inner demons become so inflamed by our culture's "contemporary propaganda for lust" that it makes us feel "that the desires we are resisting are so 'natural,' so 'healthy,' and so reasonable, that it is almost perverse and abnormal to resist them. Poster after poster, film after film, novel after novel, associate the idea of sexual indulgence with the ideas of health, normality, youth, frankness, and good humor. Now this association is a lie."[52] Behind every temptation is a lie from the pit of hell. Don't buy into it!

Paul instructs us to "take captive every thought to make it obedient to Christ" (2 Cor. 10:5). This means that every bad attitude, every ungodly motive, every thought that isn't from

God needs to be taken captive to the obedience of Christ. Writing in the seventeenth century, Puritan author William Gurnall gives us this time-proven advice: "Christian, this is imperative for you to realize: When wicked or unclean thoughts first force their way into your mind, you have not yet sinned. This is the work of the Devil. But if you so much as offer them a chair and begin polite conversation with them, you have become his accomplice. In only a short time you will give these thoughts sanctuary in your heart. Your resolve—not to yield to a temptation you are already entertaining—is no match for Satan and the longings of the flesh."[53]

Instead of entertaining sinful thoughts, we need to bring them to the Lord right away.

2. COUNTER WITH TRUTH

Jesus resisted the attacks of the Evil One with truth—specifically, biblical truth. In the same way, we need to counter wrongful thoughts with the powerful truth of God's Word. Our counterattack may be something we say out loud or to ourselves, or it might take the form of a prayer. As Jesus clearly demonstrates, we must oppose sinful ways of thinking by either quoting Scripture verbatim or bringing biblical truth to bear on our situation.

It is imperative, therefore, that we know Scripture. Jerry Bridges contends that "if we truly desire to live in the realm of the Spirit, we must continually feed our minds with his truth. It is hypocritical to pray for victory over our sins yet be careless in our intake of the word of God."[54] A working knowledge of the Bible is a must for doing spiritual battle.

The psalmist strived to hide God's Word in his heart to keep from sinning against the Lord (Ps. 119:11). The best way to hide the Word of God in our hearts is to memorize it. Having Scripture verses stored in our hearts and minds allows us to draw strength and power from God's Word when we face temptation.

3. RENOUNCE SIN

Enticing as Satan's offers were, Jesus rejected them, which is something we need to do when facing temptation. Because we're constantly contending with our old nature, sin can sometimes look good to us. We may have second thoughts as to whether certain negative behavior is really all that bad. We may even choose to tolerate it—try to manage it so it doesn't get too far out of control, but not eradicate it. Instead of compromising, we need to follow Jesus' example and renounce sin whenever the Holy Spirit brings it to light. Renouncing sin simply means that we forsake it. We say either out loud or silently, to God and to ourselves, that the sin we're contemplating is wrong. We remind ourselves that no matter how tempting it is, sin jeopardizes our ministry, our relationships with others, and our relationship with God.

Sin never satisfies. It always leaves us empty and destitute. The more you tell yourself that something is not good for you, the more your whole body will believe it, and it will eventually lose its grip on you. Satan tries to make bad things look good to us and good things look bad. He is the father of lies (John 8:44), so when we renounce sin, we strike a major blow in his continuing efforts to deceive us.

The early Christians had a good understanding of the importance of renouncing sin. In the ancient Christian baptismal liturgy, candidates were asked three important questions: "Do you renounce Satan and all the spiritual forces of wickedness that rebel against God? Do you renounce the evil powers of this world that corrupt and destroy the creatures of God? Do you renounce all sinful desires that draw you from the love of God?" Of course, the proper response in each case was, "Yes, I renounce them!"

Adam and Eve

Let's contrast how Jesus responded to Satan with how Adam and Eve reacted (Gen. 3:1–7; see fig. 2), which closely resembles how human beings most often handle temptation. The first thing Satan said to Eve was, in effect, "You poor woman. God said you couldn't eat from any of these

FIG. 2

Satan Tempting Eve

Genesis 3:1–7

fine-looking trees here in the garden." That, of course, was a lie. God didn't say to stay away from all the trees, just one. Satan often tries to get us to focus our attention on what we don't have as opposed to all we do have.

In her response, Eve minimized the importance of the tree, in much the same way we minimize sin, making it sound as if it's no big deal. Instead of referring to it as the tree of the knowledge of good and evil, she said something like, "Yeah, God said to stay away from some tree in the middle of the garden or we'll die."

"You're not gonna die!" Satan assured her. "That God of yours is a killjoy! He's withholding wonderful things from you because he doesn't want you to be like him. Go ahead. Nothing bad will happen." That's just like Satan, isn't it? He tries to distort our concept of who God is. He tries to get us to believe that God doesn't love us or care about us and that God is being unfair. The Evil One also wants us to think that our bad behavior is no big deal, that it certainly isn't going to hurt anything.

Adam, by the way, didn't fare any better than his wife. The Bible records no dialogue between him and Satan. It appears Adam didn't put up much of a fight. He gave in willingly and impulsively. So how would you evaluate how well Adam and Eve handled the temptation? First, did they counter quickly? Eve did initially, but it was downhill from there. They were not persistent in countering with truth, and they never reached a point where they renounced sin and said, "No, this is wrong!"

Application to Real-Life Situations

Before we come down too hard on Adam and Eve, let's put ourselves in some common situations we face and see how we do. Figure 3 deals with some of the thoughts leading to the sin of bitterness. Notice that the right side is blank. No comebacks. No responses. No standing up to temptation. Unfortunately, that's how it often goes when ungodly thoughts pop into our minds. Like Adam, we don't put up any fight. Instead of taking every thought captive to the obedience of Christ, we all too often toy with wrongful thoughts.

Fill in the right side of figure 3, keeping in mind the need to counter quickly, counter with truth, and renounce sin. You can do this as a group, with friends, or by yourself. Then do the same for figure 4, which deals with lust, and figure 5, which focuses on envy. Figure 6 presents a particularly challenging temptation for modern Christians: pornography. I took a stab at filling in the blanks in figures 7–10 at the end of the chapter, but remember, there is no set way of responding. My version is just one example. Everyone will have a different approach from one situation to another.

FIG. 3

Doing Spiritual Battle against Bitterness

FIG. 4

Doing Spiritual Battle against Lust

FIG. 5

Doing Spiritual Battle against Envy

FIG. 6

Doing Spiritual Battle against Pornography

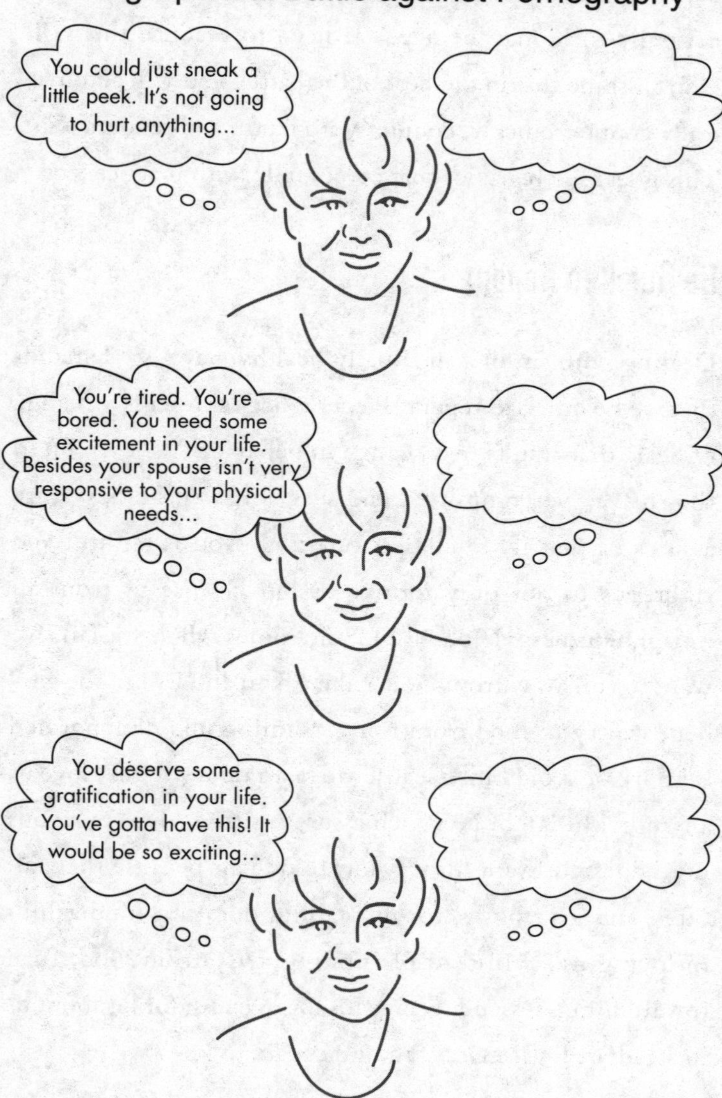

The reason I include these worksheets is because taking every thought captive to the obedience of Christ doesn't come naturally to human beings. We need to practice this skill. Don't assume that in the heat of the battle, you will automatically counter quickly, counter with truth, and renounce sin. This is learned behavior that comes only with practice.

Be Quick to Repent

Dealing with sin in a spiritually healthy way also demands that we be quick to repent. Repentance represents a change of heart that results in a change in behavior. We own up to the sins we've committed and seek forgiveness. Scripture assures us that if we confess our sins, God is faithful and righteous to not only forgive us but cleanse us from all unrighteousness (1 John 1:9). Sometimes when we fail, we want to run away from God. Like Adam and Eve in the garden, we try to hide from him, assuming he's disappointed with us, or avoid him because we're afraid he doesn't love us anymore. Julian of Norwich assures us that "our courteous Lord does not want his servants to despair because they fall often and grievously; for our falling does not hinder him in loving us."[55] Instead of running away from God, turn toward him, seek and receive his forgiveness, for he abounds in steadfast love, mercy, and grace (Ex. 34:6–7).

Why Do You Obey Christ?

I've heard chaplains for sports teams say that athletes are more spiritual when they are injured. The injury puts their careers in jeopardy, so they faithfully attend Bible studies and prayer groups because they're desperate. When they heal and resume playing, they pretty much forget about God and go back to the way they used to live. That's a generalization, of course, but we artists need to face the fact that we too can be fair-weather Christians, committed when we need God to do something for us but flagging in devotion the rest of the time.

I'd like to zero in on a question facing those in worship ministry, as well as all Christians in the creative and performing arts. The question is, why do you live a godly life? What motivates you to obey Christ? Why are you "good"? When I pressed myself to be honest about it, I realized there are parts of me that obey because I want God to help me write a great worship song. Or I want some artist to follow through on their interest in recording my song. Or I want Sunday's service to be stellar.

I'm not saying it's wrong to obey because we want God's fullest blessing on our lives. But in my case, I was treating obedience (and God) as a means to an end. When I wanted something from God, I was a "good boy." But when God didn't answer my prayer or when things didn't go my way, my obedience wavered. Again, I'm not trying to challenge the notion that we need to abide in Christ if we minister in his name. And of course if God is going to use us to our fullest, we need to live lives of obedience and trust. I'm simply asking, what's driving our obedience?

In John 14:21, Jesus says, "Whoever has my commands and keeps them is the one who loves me." For too long I read that verse and concluded that I needed to try harder to be a better Christian. But there's a deeper truth in this verse. Jesus is inviting us to love him more and to allow our obedience to flow out of that love. In John 14:15, Jesus reiterates the relationship between love and obedience: "If you love me, you will obey what I command" (NIV 1984). Jesus establishes a cause-and-effect relationship between our love for him and our obedience, which prompts numerous questions. Do you obey God because you love Jesus, or because you love using the gifts and talents he gave you? Would you continue to have devotions or even care about spiritual things if you couldn't write, create, or perform? Do you love leading worship, performing, writing, or creating more than you love Christ?

Enjoying the Gifts More Than the Giver

I love to write music. The creative process energizes me. I feel most alive when I'm working on a song. There were times, though, when I wondered whether I loved writing music more than I loved Jesus. This question came to the forefront several years ago during a two-year period in which I didn't write a single song. My responsibilities at the church were such that I didn't have time to write. Song ideas would pop into my head, but I wasn't able to develop them. I felt like an injured athlete watching the game from the sidelines instead of playing. I wondered whether I would ever write again. I struggled in my relationship with God, and I must admit that there were times when the day-to-day challenges of living in obedience to Christ were met with, "Why, what's the use?"

Then one night something touched me deeply during a worship time at church, and I wept as I drove home. I realized that I had been taking Jesus for granted. I told the Lord that if I never wrote again, that would be difficult, but I'd be okay because I would always have him. That was not an easy thing for me to say, but being unable to write for two years boiled life down to the basics. I came to the point where I was desperately hungry for God, much as the psalmist was when he wrote, "As the deer pants for streams of water, so my soul pants for you, my God" (Ps. 42:1).

Things that I thought I couldn't live without (such as music) now paled in comparison with knowing Christ. Paul says, "I consider everything a loss because of the surpassing worth of knowing Christ Jesus my Lord, for whose sake I have lost all things. I consider them garbage, that I may gain Christ" (Phil. 3:8). I thought I valued knowing Christ more than I valued music, but I really didn't. My passion for my work, for ministry, was greater than my passion for God. My obedience to the Lord was motivated more by the thrill of doing music for church than by a sincere love for Jesus. Is it okay to love music? Is it okay to love leading people in worship? Of course it is. God gifted us and called us into ministry. But in my case, I loved the blessings of God—a secure job, a chance to write music, and a certain amount of notoriety—more than I loved God. I was enjoying the gifts more than the Giver.

I repented of my shallow and selfish religiosity and told the Lord that if he would allow me to write again (which he did), I would never again take him for granted. I also asked Jesus to deepen my love for him. It was another one of my daily dangerous prayers. For two years, I prayed every day for God to help me love Jesus more. I beseeched the Lord to help me love what Jesus loves and love others as Jesus loves them. I begged God to break me of my fair-weather obedience so I could obey freely and naturally out of a sincere love for Jesus.

The Bigger Payoff

During my two-year hiatus from songwriting, I discovered the hidden benefit of obedience, which is found in the second half of John 14:21: "The one who loves me will be loved by my Father, and I too will love them and show myself to them." The greatest payoff of obedience is intimacy with God. When we obey, we fall deeper in love with Jesus and he reveals more of himself to us. "Blessed are the pure in heart, for they will see God" (Matt. 5:8). Obedience enables us to experience more of God in our lives.

Recognizing intimacy with God as the ultimate benefit of obedience brought other pertinent questions to the surface. Do I really want to be more intimate with God? Is that really what I want out of life? Or would I rather be a successful, famous songwriter? Having put my talent on the altar, the choice was now easy: I want Jesus more than anything else. My desert experience taught me that I can live without music, but I can't live without Jesus.

FIG. 7

Possible Responses to Bitterness

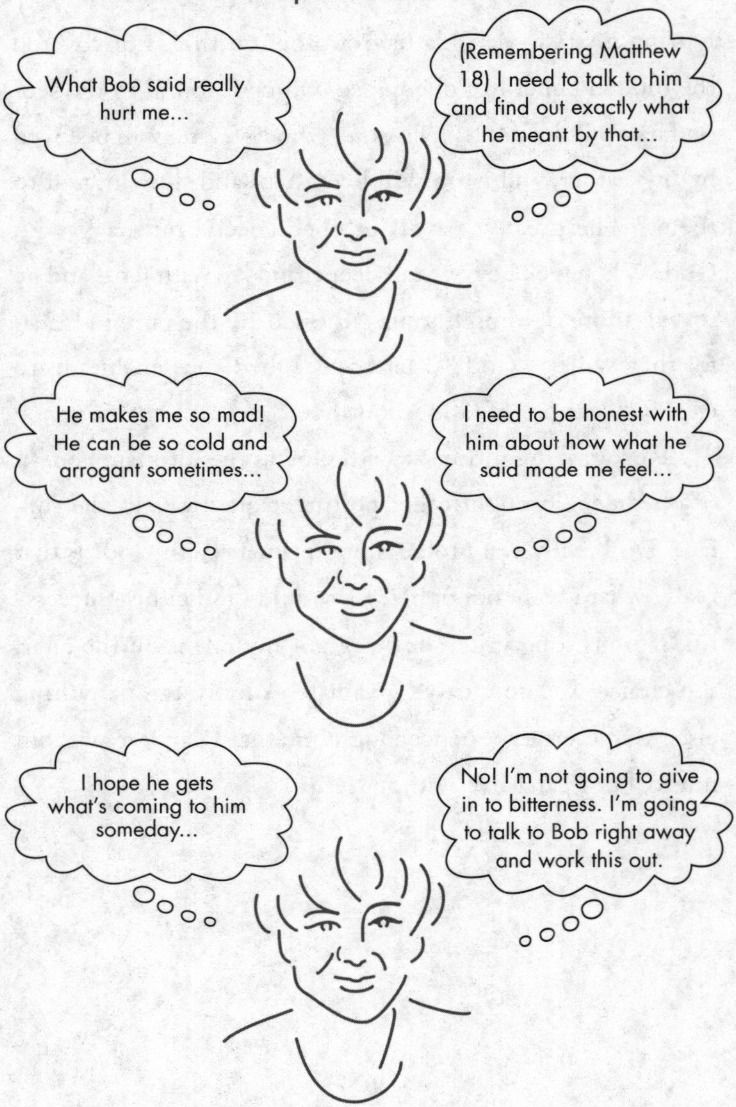

What Bob said really hurt me...

(Remembering Matthew 18) I need to talk to him and find out exactly what he meant by that...

He makes me so mad! He can be so cold and arrogant sometimes...

I need to be honest with him about how what he said made me feel...

I hope he gets what's coming to him someday...

No! I'm not going to give in to bitterness. I'm going to talk to Bob right away and work this out.

FIG. 8

Possible Responses to Lust

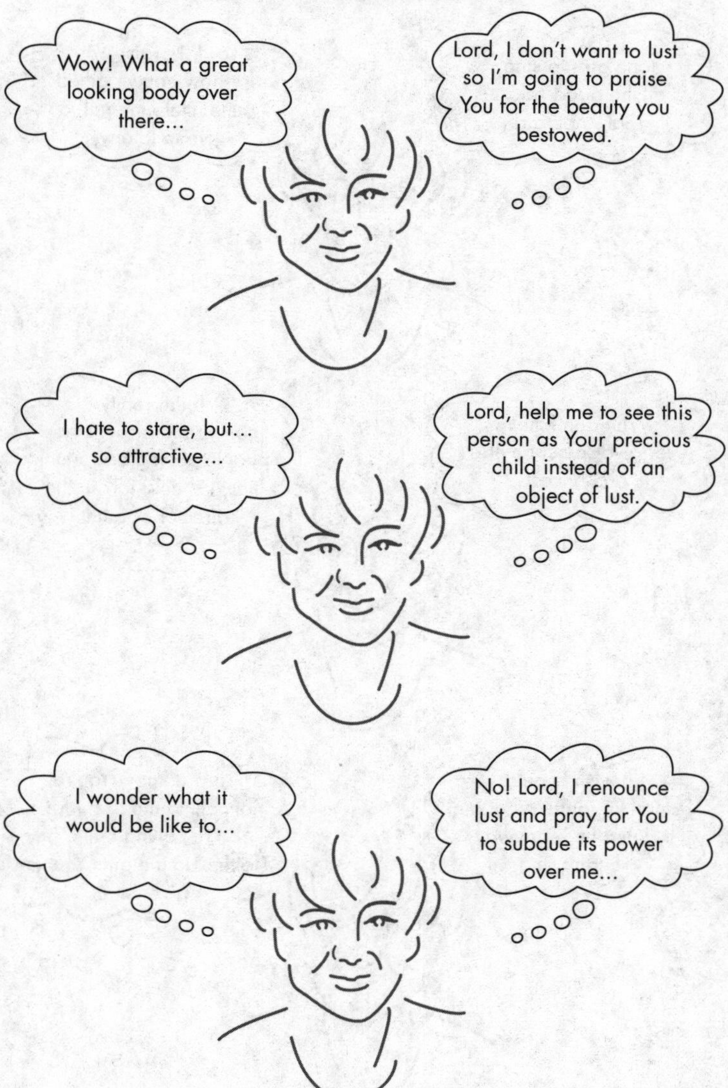

FIG. 9

Possible Responses to Envy

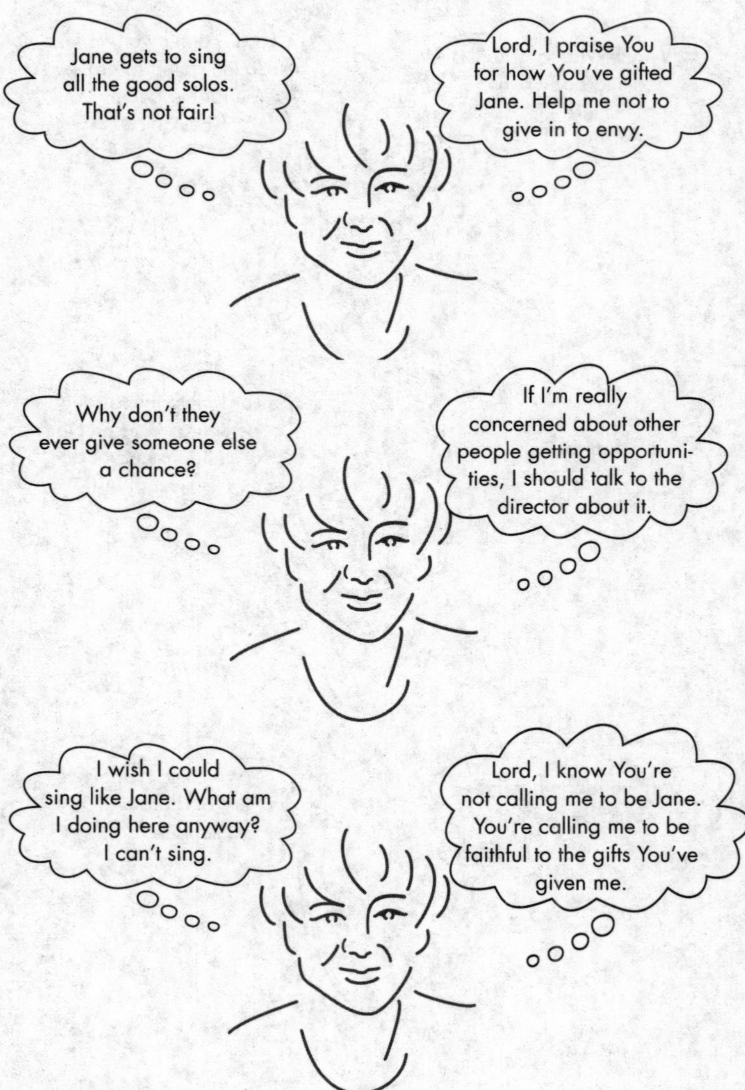

FIG. 10

Possible Responses to Pornography

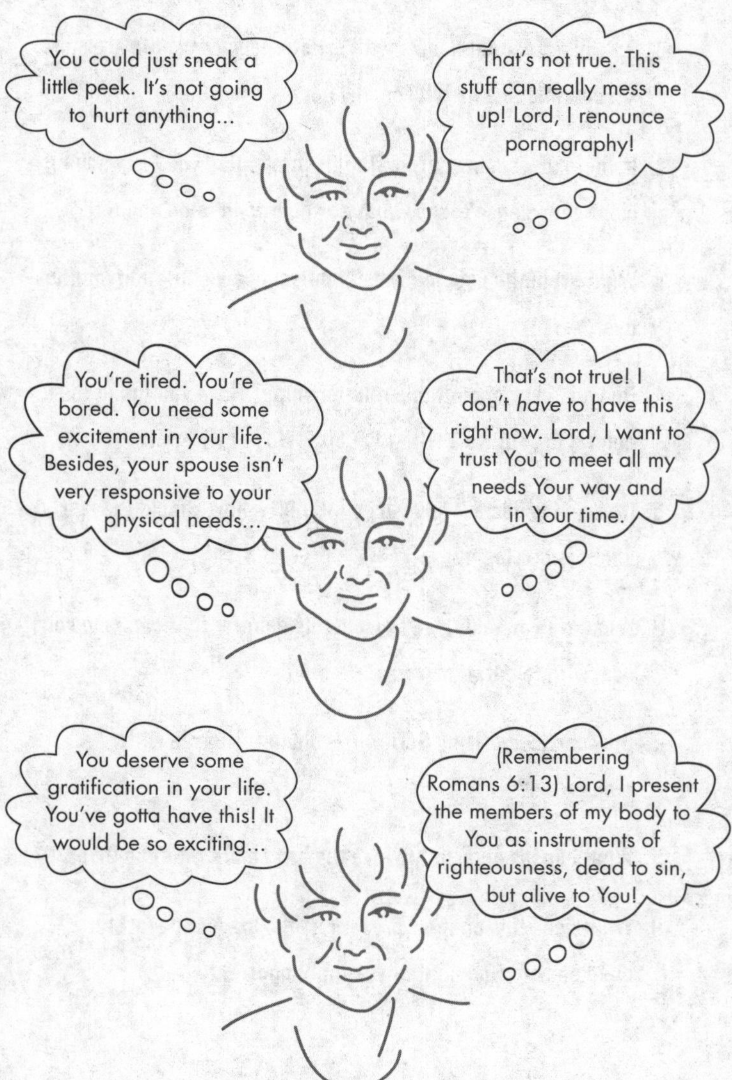

Follow-Up Questions for Group Discussion

1. Do you agree that people with artistic temperaments are more susceptible to sin? Why or why not?
2. Is there any sin in your life that is preventing you from having a clear conscience? If so, what do you intend to do about it?
3. What prohibits people from establishing accountability in their lives?
4. Do you have accountable relationships? Have you found them helpful in your walk with the Lord? Why or why not?
5. If someone doesn't have accountability, how should they go about acquiring it?
6. What are you taking away from this chapter that can help you deal with temptation?
7. How can memorizing Scripture help in the battle with temptation?
8. What causes an artist to love the gifts more than the Giver?
9. What does this chapter present as the biggest payoff for obedience to God, and why is that important?

PERSONAL ACTION STEPS

1. If you don't have accountability right now, find someone with whom you could initiate such a relationship. Set up a meeting with that person and ask him or her to hold you accountable regarding the areas of potential sin in your life.

2. If you do have an accountable relationship with someone right now, evaluate how it's going. Are the two of you being completely honest with each other about your struggles? What changes could be made to improve accountability?

3. Identify the temptation to which you are most vulnerable and determine what it means to counter quickly, counter with truth, and renounce sin when you face this temptation. Using figure 11, on the left put the thoughts that pop into your mind when you're tempted, and on the right write appropriate responses based on truth.

4. Memorize at least three Scripture passages to help you deal with the temptations you face most often.

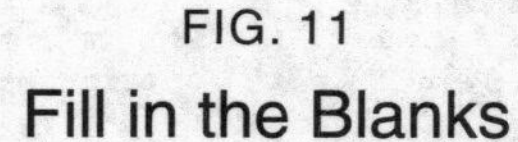

FIG. 11

Fill in the Blanks

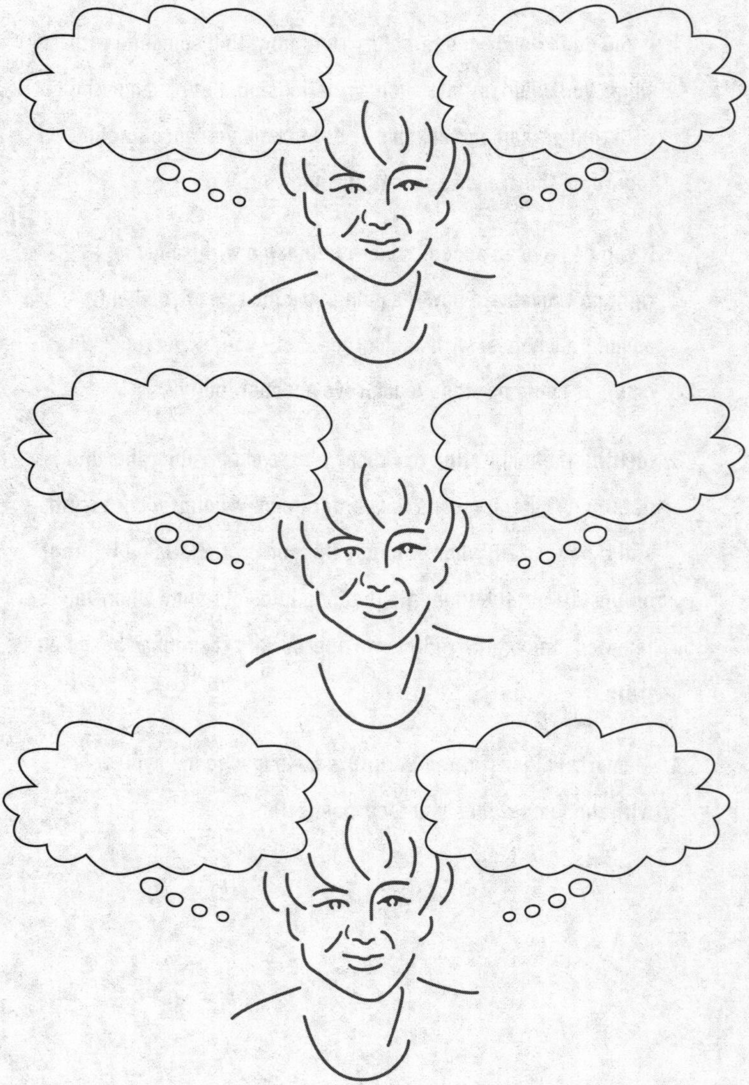

CHAPTER 10

THE SPIRITUAL DISCIPLINES OF THE ARTIST

KYRA IS AN INTERNATIONALLY ACCLAIMED POET and is recognized as one of the leading writers of her generation. She rose to fame overnight with a collection of poems titled *Death and Life in the Garden*. It's been almost five years since *Death and Life* hit the *New York Times* bestseller list, and since then Kyra has been on the fast track, reaping the fruits of her success. The lecture circuit, book deals, job offers, and command performances for the president have kept her extremely busy these last several years. This is what she's dreamed about since she started writing poetry in high school.

Tonight, though, as Kyra drives back to her hotel room after speaking at another literary convention, she's about as low as she's ever been in her life. She knows something's not right with her. Feelings of anxiety and emptiness have been gnawing at her for some time now. She felt a tinge of anger when a reporter from a local newspaper asked, "What have you written since *Death and Life*?" It was an innocent question, and one she's been asked before. But this time the question irritated her. She responded by mumbling something about being busy with another collection of poems to be released next year. That's a half-truth. Or a half-lie, depending on how you look at it. She has a book deadline that's been moved to next year after having been moved five previous times. The truth is, she hasn't even started the new book.

Kyra has been telling herself for a while now that she doesn't have time to write anymore, but as she drags her tired body back to the hotel this cold winter evening, she knows that's just an excuse. She's written bits and pieces on planes and in hotel restaurants, but she knows it's not the same caliber as *Death and Life*. It's not for lack of time that her work has suffered. She fears that she's lost it, although she doesn't know what it is, whether it's her ability, her edge, or her verve. "Kyra has gained the literary world and lost her soulish voice," one of the critics wrote recently. Kyra was troubled and angry when she read that review, but she knows it's true. You see, Kyra is a committed Christian who used to spend a lot of quality time with the Lord.

Even though *Death and Life* is not a religious work, it has spiritual overtones. And Kyra knows that it grew out of her times of solitude with her Lord and Savior. She knows full well that her quiet times, as she calls them, enabled her to listen to God and hear the deeper truths of his Word. During those times of solitude, Kyra got in touch with her deepest feelings, especially her inner despair. She felt safe and secure in God's presence. She also gained greater empathy for others who struggle and was able to identify with all who suffer. Her ability to enter into the plight of fellow human beings added depth and richness to her writing.

Kyra fights back tears as she sits in her hotel room. She misses that old rocking chair by the fireplace at her parent's house. While growing up, she sat in that chair every morning, reading her Bible and praying. She felt like God was right there in the room, sitting beside her, speaking to her through his Word, listening as she prayed. She used to journal about what God was doing in her life; sometimes she'd lose track of time and write for hours on end. She felt connected to God back then, more in tune with the stirrings of her soul. It dawns on her that it's not that old rocking chair that she misses. *How did I end up so far from God?* she wonders. She begins to pray and for some reason feels compelled to pray out loud. She lifts up her eyes and cries out, "Lord, I feel so far away from you right now . . ."

Suddenly her phone rings. On the other end is a radio

talk show host. Kyra immediately remembers she agreed to do a live interview after her speech this evening. Within twenty seconds, she's on the air live over a Christian radio network. Though she's tired, Kyra manages to catch her second wind, do the interview, and even take a few calls from listeners. Off the air the host thanks her for her time, expresses admiration for her work, and closes by saying, "Kyra, you are an inspiration to all of us. Whenever I read *Death and Life*, I feel as if I'm reading the journal of someone who walks close to God. I wish I were more like you." Kyra cringes and feels like the biggest hypocrite. She hangs up and cries herself to sleep.

Questions for Group Discussion

1. Why were those quiet times Kyra spent with the Lord so significant for her?
2. If Kyra's quiet times meant so much to her, why weren't they part of her regular routine anymore?
3. How would you counsel someone like Kyra who feels disconnected from the Lord?
4. What percentage of Christians would you guess have regular devotions?

5. What, in your opinion, keeps Christians from consistently spending personal time with the Lord?
6. Do you think it's important for artists to have regular quiet times? Why or why not?
7. How might hypocrisy or duplicity manifest itself in the life of a worship leader or church artist?
8. What spiritual disciplines would you recommend artists practice regularly?

Are We Really That Undisciplined?

I had an interesting discussion with a professional counselor who pointed out that his experience with people with artistic temperaments was that they are highly undisciplined. He referred to us as free spirits who are usually messy, unorganized, always late for appointments, and irresponsible with personal finances. Is that true? Do you think artists are undisciplined people?

I, for one, don't agree. Think about all that's involved in becoming an accomplished artist. It takes a lot of hard work. Thousands of hours of practice. It takes—you guessed it—discipline. Consider all the rehearsing and training that goes into being an artist. One study of musicians revealed that by the age of twenty-one, "a talented pupil will have spent about 10,000 hours in purposeful practice."[56] There's no denying that being an artist calls for an unusual amount of discipline. Why do some parents insist that their kids take piano lessons? For the discipline. Artists pour large amounts of time and effort into developing their talents.

Who understands the value of discipline more than artists? You wouldn't attempt to play a violin concerto or sing an aria without disciplined practice. You'd never try to act the lead in a play without memorizing lines and knowing your blocking. If you want to achieve anything in the arts, it takes concerted study, training, and practice. Artists know from firsthand experience that discipline reaps rewards and allows us to do things we couldn't otherwise do. Discipline is hard work, but it pays off.

The same truth applies to the spiritual life. That's why Paul tells Timothy, "Train yourself to be godly. For physical training is of some value, but godliness has value for all things, holding promise for both the present life and the life to come" (1 Tim. 4:7–8). Spiritual disciplines pay dividends for all of this life as well as for the next. Solitude, Bible reading, prayer, fasting, Scripture memorization—all have long-lasting, far-reaching benefits. Paul uses a sports analogy to show how discipline works in the spiritual life. "Do you not know that in a race all the runners run, but only one gets the prize? Run in such a way as to get the prize. Everyone who competes in the games goes into strict training. They do it to get a crown that will not last, but we do it to get a crown that will last forever. Therefore I do not run like someone running aimlessly; I do not fight like a boxer beating the air. No, I strike a blow to my body and make it my slave so that after I have preached to others, I myself will not be disqualified for the prize" (1 Cor. 9:24–27).

You will not grow spiritually and be everything God wants you to be without a modest amount of self-discipline.

Even though I portray artists as being amenable to discipline, I can't deny the stereotype, to which my counselor friend alluded, that artists can be rather undisciplined. We tend to be selective with our efforts, working conscientiously to develop our talents but letting other, more mundane responsibilities slide. Sometimes simple activities like balancing our checkbooks or following through on emails and phone calls fall off the radar. In addition to developing our talents and tending to our basic adult responsibilities, we need to be faithful in the spiritual disciplines.

My Ministry Is the Product of My Relationship with Christ

Early in my ministry, I learned a valuable principle that has helped shape my priorities throughout my life. I was taught that my ministry is the product of my relationship with

Christ. Jesus invites us to abide in him. "Remain in me, as I also remain in you. No branch can bear fruit by itself; it must remain in the vine. Neither can you bear fruit unless you remain in me. I am the vine; you are the branches. If you remain in me and I in you, you will bear much fruit; apart from me you can do nothing" (John 15:4–5). Abiding in Christ means that we are in right relationship with him, that we're growing in him, that our lives reflect his love, and that our hearts are full of his Word.

Ministry that flows out of an abiding relationship with Jesus is authentic and dynamic. In Colossians 3:16, notice that ministry in the arts comes after we're filled with God's Word: "Let the message of Christ dwell among you richly as you teach and admonish one another with all wisdom through psalms, hymns, and songs from the Spirit, singing to God with gratitude in your hearts." If you abide in Christ, psalms, hymns, and spiritual songs will flow naturally and abundantly out of your soul.

We're missing something if we think all we have to do to have an effective ministry for Christ is be a great singer or worship leader. There's so much more to it than that. There is a correlation between knowing God and bearing fruit. Ministry is most powerful when it emanates from a life spent in intimate fellowship with the Father. You can tell when someone spends time with God. His or her ministry bears fruit in a deeply spiritual and powerful way. The older I get, the less impressed I am with flash and glitz, and the more I'm drawn to men and women who spend time with God. Their ministry is indeed the product of their relationship with Christ. They fellowship with the Lord and it shows, for they minister powerfully in the Spirit. Before the disciples went out to minister, they spent time with Jesus (Matt. 10:5–42). Their ministry flowed out of their relationship with Christ.

I have discovered that this principle applies to other areas of my life as well. My parenting is the product of my relationship with Christ. I can't strive to be an involved and loving father without regular fellowship with my compassionate and gracious heavenly Father. My marriage is the product of my relationship with Christ. I can't love my wife as Christ loves the church unless I'm in daily contact with Jesus. Colossians 1:10 tells us to "live a life worthy of the Lord and please him in every way: bearing fruit in every good work, growing in the knowledge of God." Spending time at the feet of Jesus enables us to bear fruit in every part of our lives.

George Frederic Handel was a deeply spiritual man who walked with Christ. As he wrote the glorious "Hallelujah" chorus, he broke down in tears and cried out, "I did think I did see all heaven before me, and the great God himself."[57] But today, except in rare cases, when the "Hallelujah" chorus is performed, we focus on the choir, the soloists, the orchestra, the conductor, the period or nonperiod instruments, the recording, the acoustics—everything but God himself. I'm not referring just to the audience and critics. The musicians can be equally as guilty of fixating on the music so much that they miss the gospel message behind the entire oratorio. We Christian artists can fall into the same trap of doing religious music or worship music detached from Christ.

Fellowshiping with God

God desires intimate fellowship with us (1 Cor. 1:9). He is not far away and aloof; God is near and draws even closer when we draw near to him (Jer. 23:23; James 4:8). Paul reminds us in his letter to the Corinthians that God wants to dwell in us and walk among us, that God regards us as his own and welcomes us into his presence, and that God purposes to relate to us as a loving father (2 Cor. 6:16–18). We belong to God and he belongs to us; we are his and he is our God. The God of the universe is a deeply relational being who enjoys spending personal time with each of us.

The question is not whether God wants to be in relationship with us; the question is whether we truly desire fellowship with him. The problem, as Jack Deere sees it, is that God wants a relationship, but we'd rather have results; God wants to talk, but we'd prefer that he solve our problems or make us successful.[58] To fellowship with God requires that we respond to the invitation to enter into loving communion with him.

Jesus calls us friends (John 15:14–15). But as we all know, friendships don't happen without intentionality. Friends spend time together. They enjoy each other's company. They know a lot about each other because they get together regularly. "Real friendships," observes Deere, "can't be forced. They must be chosen, and then pursued."[59] Friendships grow when both parties commit to being in relationship with each other.

Intimate fellowship with God and with his Son, Jesus Christ, is a great privilege with far-reaching benefits. God really does reward those who earnestly seek him (Heb. 11:6; Deut. 4:29). We can turn to him in times of need and go to him for guidance and counsel. We can share our joy with him as well as our pain and sorrow. The privilege of fellowshiping with God prompted the psalmist to proclaim, "As for me, it is good to be near God" (Ps. 73:28).

Knowing Christ

Paul asserts that knowing God in Christ is more important than anything else. "I consider everything a loss because of the surpassing worth of knowing Christ Jesus my Lord, for whose sake I have lost all things. I consider them garbage, that I may gain Christ" (Phil. 3:8). Experiencing intimacy with God was top priority for David. "One thing I ask from the LORD, this only do I seek: that I may dwell in the house of the LORD all the days of my life, to gaze on the beauty of the LORD and to seek him in his temple" (Ps. 27:4). Knowing God is the goal of eternal life (John 17:3); we've been redeemed so we can live in loving communion with the Lord for all eternity.

Knowing God is even more important than being a successful worship leader or artist. In Jeremiah 9:23–24, God told the people of Israel to boast not about having wisdom, power, or riches but about knowing him. Let's consider what God's admonishment would sound like if set in the context of a worship ministry: "'Let not the musicians boast about their music, let not the tech team brag about its stellar productions, and let not the visual artists boast about the stunning art display in the lobby. But let those who boast, boast that they understand and know me, that I am the Lord, who exercises kindness, justice, and righteousness on earth, for I delight in these things,' declares the Lord."

Life's highest priority is not our art but our relationship with God.

In his classic work on this topic, J. I. Packer extols the value of knowing God. "What were we made for? To know God. What aim should we set ourselves in life? To know God. . . . What is the best thing in life, bringing more joy, delight, and contentment, than anything else? Knowledge of God."[60]

Philip was the disciple who said to Jesus, "Lord, show

us the Father and that will be enough for us" (John 14:8). Jesus sounds a little frustrated with Philip when he replies, "Don't you know me, Philip, even after I have been among you such a long time? Anyone who has seen me has seen the Father. How can you say, 'Show us the Father'?" (v. 9). Even though Philip hung out with Jesus and the other disciples, he didn't know Jesus. Sadly, too many Christians are religious, maybe even involved at church, but they still don't know Christ because they've never truly cultivated a relationship with God.

Nurturing a Relationship

If my ministry is the product of my relationship with Christ, I need to nurture that relationship. The best way I've found to nurture a friendship with God is to have a regular quiet time. When I talk about having a quiet time, I'm referring to a block of time set aside consistently for Bible reading and prayer. Some might call this devotions; others might refer to it as their daily appointment with God. It doesn't matter what we call it; what matters is that we engage with the Lord on a regular basis.

While in school, I was accountable to a group of friends about having regular quiet times. Playing off the idea that a quiet time provides food for the soul, we'd ask, "What did you have for breakfast?" when greeting each other at school every day. Of course, what we were really asking was, "Did you have your quiet time this morning?" One of the reasons I developed this discipline early in life was because I knew I was going to run into somebody at school who was going to ask me about it.

I know this can be a touchy subject with Christians. People often feel guilty when I bring up the topic of private devotions. I stopped teaching about it for a season because I assumed everyone's already heard about it and is practicing regular quiet times. But the truth is, we're not. Having devotions is like flossing. It's something we all know we're supposed to do every day, but few people actually do it. And I'm not saying you're a bad Christian if you don't have a consistent quiet time. I'm not out to lay a guilt trip on anyone; some of you already feel embarrassed or ashamed anytime this subject comes up. You've tried to have regular devotions but weren't able to be consistent with it. You might even be thinking God is holding a grudge against you because you missed a few quiet times.

Friends, I invite you to get out of that vicious cycle. That guilt trip is not from God. That's from the Evil One, who constantly accuses and criticizes us (Rev. 12:10). His strategy is to beat you down and keep you as far away from God as possible. Don't let him win! God is not shaking his fist in anger because you're not having devotions. God doesn't look at you and say, "You're so undisciplined. What's wrong with you? Get your act together, or I'm gonna stop loving you." God is not like that. You are his beloved child. He looks at you with infinite tenderness and says, "Come to me. Let's spend some time together. I want to be close to you." Your heavenly Father is always inviting you into deeper levels of intimacy with him. How are you responding to that invitation?

My Personal Lifeline

I've come to the conclusion that my quiet time is the most important appointment of my day. Direction for my life, vision for my ministry, Scriptures to help with temptation, even song ideas have all come out of my times of solitude with the Lord. I don't mean to sound dramatic, but I don't think I could live without God's Word. I certainly don't know where I would be if it weren't for my quiet times with the Lord. Moses said that God's words "are not just idle words for you—they are your life" (Deut. 32:47). I've come to view my quiet time as my lifeline.

I need time with the Lord because I know that apart from him I can do nothing (John 15:5). I need his wisdom and strength. I need his guidance and direction. In their classic book *Experiencing God*, Henry Blackaby and Claude King encourage us to spend time with the Lord, find out what he's doing in and around us, and then adjust our lives to be a part of that. "Right now God is working all around you and in your life. . . . The Holy Spirit and the Word of God will instruct you and help you know when and where God is working. Once you know where he is working, you can adjust your life to join him where he is working. Once you join God in what he is doing you will experience him accomplishing his activity through your life. When you enter this kind of intimate love relationship with God, you will know and do the will of God and experience him in ways you have never known before. Only God can bring you into that kind of relationship, but he stands ready to do so."[61]

It is regular fellowship with God, not doing life and ministry by our own power, that keeps us in touch with God's ongoing work in our midst. I don't understand how non-Christians can live without Christ, but I'm completely baffled as to why Christians would try to live without him. I can't comprehend why someone would make a commitment to follow Jesus but not spend time with him. I feel so strongly about this that if I were on my deathbed, my last words of advice to anyone who would listen would be, "Spend time with the Lord." It's the greatest privilege in all of life.

Where Our Character Is Formed

My quiet times have also been instrumental in shaping my character. Scripture indicates that God is the one who initiates and carries out our spiritual development (Phil. 1:6; 2:13). God has used those private times with him to grow me up spiritually. When I told my spiritual mentor, John Allen, whom I described in chapter 2, that I seriously wanted to grow in godly character, his response was, "Good. I'll pray that God sends difficulty into your life to make you grow." Thanks a lot, John! I've since learned that God often uses the problems we face and the difficulties we encounter to mold our character. He does so out of love; the Lord "disciplines the one he loves" (Heb. 12:6). My character has been shaped—and continues to be shaped—in the context of a loving relationship with God through Jesus Christ.

I don't know how many times I've said, "God, I'm weak in this area. Help me grow." Scripture says we are to "grow up in all aspects" (Eph. 4:15 NASB). What better place to grow as a person and as a believer than within the safety of an intimate relationship with the God who made us and knows us better than we know ourselves? I sought God's wisdom for dealing with my perfectionism. Sometimes the growth process felt like surgery. The Holy Spirit would point out my perfectionistic behavior and lovingly say, "This has got to go." Sometimes it felt like therapy as I shared my struggles with the Lord and asked, "How do you want me to respond in this situation? How do you want me to address this issue?" Many times he then led me to something in his Word that either ministered deeply to my soul or spoke directly to my problem. Genuine spiritual transformation occurs most effectively in the context of a loving, growing, and intimately personal relationship with the Lord.

Bible Study and Prayer

The first Christians devoted themselves to Bible study and prayer (Acts 6:4). Since the beginning of our faith, these two practices have been foundational to the Christian life. Reading God's Word and praying are more than classic spiritual disciplines; they're proven ways to cultivate intimacy with God.

IMMERSE YOURSELF IN GOD'S WORD

Second Timothy 3:16–17 teaches that all Scripture "is useful for teaching, rebuking, correcting and training in righteousness, so that the servant of God may be thoroughly equipped for every good work." God uses Scripture to train us and equip us to do what he's called us to do. Bible study plays a vital role in our training as artists in the church.

God told Jeremiah that he would put his words in the prophet's mouth (Jer. 1:9). Jeremiah spoke on behalf of God; he was in a sense God's mouthpiece. We artists in the church represent the Lord in much the same way. The words we sing, our prayers, our comments put us in position to be God's mouthpiece. I hope we never take that responsibility lightly. If you minister in Jesus' name, you need to immerse yourself in Scripture so you can communicate adequately God's words and his ways.

As God's spokespeople, you and I need to handle correctly "the word of truth" (2 Tim. 2:15). We must be able to discern biblical truth. When I run across a song lyric that contradicts Scripture, it tells me that the writer or performer either doesn't know the Bible or is not committed to representing God accurately. We need to be students of God's Word so we can discern what is scriptural and what is not. Those involved in worship ministry are often approached by congregation members with questions. They see you playing guitar on the platform or sitting behind the soundboard or manning a camera and they assume you know something about the Bible and can answer their questions about God. Peter advises Christians to always be ready to respond to any inquiries about the reason behind our hope (1 Peter 3:15). If a congregation member came up to you after the service and asked a spiritual question, would you be able to direct them to a relevant Bible passage? Could you counsel someone on a basic level from Scripture? Could you lead someone to Christ using God's Word? The high-profile nature of worship ministry comes with a responsibility to know the Bible.

DISCOVER THE PRIVILEGE AND POWER OF PRAYER

Prayer is simply talking to God. Christian prayer is based on the fact that believers are in a committed relationship with God. We can talk to him as a son or daughter talks to their loving father (John 1:12; Rom. 8:15). We can speak freely and confidently to God (Eph. 3:12). Jesus invites us to ask for anything in his name. "Ask and you will receive," he says, "and your joy will be complete" (John 16:24). No topic is off-limits; no concern is too trivial. We can tell the Lord anything and everything. We can be honest about how we're feeling and pour our hearts out before him. This great privilege is not confined to the quiet time we set aside once a day. We can continue to pray anytime, anywhere, throughout our day. One of the truly unique aspects of our Judeo-Christian tradition is the approachability of our God.

I've witnessed the power of prayer throughout my life and especially in ministry. I remember working in a start-up church out west, and we desperately needed musicians to serve in our ministry. I prayed daily for God to send us quality singers and instrumentalists. After all, he owns the cattle on a thousand hills (Ps. 50:10), so I figured he could spare a few musicians and send them our way. Shortly after I began to pray, a woman at the church came up to me after a service and said that her brother was moving in from New York and that he played the trumpet. I didn't take it seriously. I never know what I'm getting into when someone approaches me like that. Everybody thinks their brother or sister or son or daughter is the greatest, right? Two weeks later this same woman stopped me after the service to tell me that her brother had moved into town and would like to audition for me, so I called him and set up a meeting.

What I heard at that audition was the best trumpet player I had ever heard. He had a great tone. He could play pop and classical. He could improvise and had played professionally with a lot of big names. The problem was that he was as far from God as you could be. He didn't know the Lord at all. The next morning as I was praying, I said, "Lord, maybe I need to be more specific. I've been praying for more musicians, and you sent me this pagan trumpet player." I sensed the Lord saying, "Yes, I know. I brought him here all the way from New York so he could find me. Are you going to invest time in him or not?"

Well, that put me in my place, so for several months I did everything I could to get alongside this guy. One time I had to visit him in jail because he had a drinking problem and got arrested for disturbing the peace. His language and behavior embarrassed me at first, but after a while I grew to love this fellow musician, and my heart began to ache for him to know Christ. My newfound friend eventually did come to the Lord, and to this day he has a wonderful music ministry in the southwestern part of the country.

Experiences like that—repeated over and over again throughout the years—have given me a deep appreciation for the power of prayer. God can literally move people across the country so they can get involved at a specific church. My experience with the trumpet player also taught me the value of listening. If I hadn't been on my knees, I never would have heard God say that he had brought this wayward musician to our ministry so we could lead him to Christ. I can't pat myself on the back for that, though, because my prayers were self-serving. I wanted God to bring me some gifted artists. My friend's sister, on the other hand, was praying for her brother to find Christ. Prayer is powerful, for our God is able to do exceedingly and abundantly beyond all we could ever dream or imagine (Eph. 3:20–21; 1 Cor. 2:9).

A TIME AND A PLACE

Many Christians start out with good intentions when it comes to their quiet times, but they're not able to stay consistent, so they give up trying. Whether you've had trouble with consistency or you're just starting out in the spiritual life, I'd like to offer a few suggestions that might help this important discipline become part of your regular routine.

First, select a time in your schedule that you can count on to be free most any given day. It doesn't matter whether it's morning, night, or afternoon; no time of day is more spiritual than another. Pick a time of day when you typically encounter the least amount of distraction. Also, be sure to make it a reasonable time frame. If ten minutes is all you can do, do that. If a half hour every other day or an hour a week is the best you can do for now, do that. Doing something is better than not doing anything, and you can always increase the time commitment once you've sustained some regularity.

When you've settled on a time, find a place. It can be a room or a chair or a couch—anything that's comfortable and private. For me, in the summer it's a wicker chair on our back patio, and in the winter it's a rocking chair by the fireplace. These are places that invite me back time and again for fellowship with my Savior. When it comes to establishing a regular quiet time, having a set time and a set place is more than half the battle.

HOW TO HAVE A QUIET TIME

As far as a framework for your devotions, there are myriad ways to go about it. You could ask your pastor or ministry leader for suggestions. There is also an ample supply of devotional books and other resources available these days. There is no set way to have a quiet time.

I usually advise those who are new at this to think of their devotions in the simplest of terms—as being with God, reading his Word, and talking to him in prayer. If you're starting out, read something from the New Testament, like one of the gospels (Matthew, Mark, Luke, or John). Read small sections at a time. Read slowly. This is not a contest to see how much you can devour in one sitting. This is your time with the Lord. Enjoy his presence and soak in all that he has for you during your time together. As you read, ask yourself, "What does this passage tell me about who God is or what God is like?" Underline verses in your Bible that are meaningful to you. If you run across something you don't understand, skip it for now and move on. You can ask someone later about it or research it another time.

After you've read a portion of Scripture, spend the remaining time in prayer. Pray about what you just read. Ask the Lord to show you how to apply it to your life. Pray for any needs you're aware of in the lives of friends and family, as well as your own needs. Be sure to keep your prayers simple. God does not require eloquence, just honesty.

I like to keep a prayer list with different items assigned to each day of the week. Other people might find that cumbersome, but it helps me stay focused as I pray. Some believers like to keep a journal in which they record what they learn from the Bible and/or keep track of their prayers. If a journal would be helpful to you, use one; if not, don't.

Finally, if prayer feels uncomfortable at first, keep at it. You'll get over that in short order. Prayer is something we learn by doing. Everyone is clumsy with it at first. J. Oswald Sanders says that "mastering the art of prayer, like any other art, will take time, and the amount of time we allocate to it will be the true measure of our conception of its importance. We always contrive to find time for that which we deem most important."[62] Prayer is a spiritual practice that is worth learning and doing.

VARIETY IS THE SPICE OF LIFE

Although it's good to have structure for your quiet times, especially for those starting out, I caution believers not to be rigid about it. Those who have been Christians for many years can get stuck reading the Bible and praying the same way all the time. Relationships thrive on variety. To nurture your relationship with the Lord, consider what you can do to breathe life into your devotions. The psalmist claimed that being in God's presence brought him great joy (Ps. 16:11). Don't let your time with the Lord become a ritualistic, joyless experience. Be flexible and be open to mixing things up from time to time.

Sometimes I'll start with prayer instead of ending with prayer, just to keep boredom from setting in. Other times I might spend the entire time in prayer or in the Word. A few times I've sensed the Lord saying, "I want you to worship me this morning," so I've grabbed my guitar and spent the entire time worshiping. One summer, my quiet times had become stale, so I took a month off and walked around a nearby lake early in the morning. As I observed the beauty of the sunrise on the water, I sensed God's presence differently than when sitting in my quiet time chair at home. Every morning, I looked forward to going for a walk with the Lord. A month later, I went back to my usual routine with renewed vigor.

Artists tend to get bored easily. We thrive on variety, innovation, and creativity. So when it comes to your devotions, feel free to change things up. Write a letter to God. Compose a song or poem, not for church but just for the Lord. Do a topical study from the Bible. Use a Bible commentary or devotional guide. A number of times I've gone through a fill-in-the-blank Bible study workbook. Don't let your quiet time become a mindless and emotionless ritual. Be open to something different in order to liven things up.

TOO BUSY?

The main reason Christians don't have a regular quiet time is that we're too busy. One morning when Martin Luther was faced with another fast-paced day, he said, "I'm too busy not to pray." So it is with us. The busier we are, the more reason we have to spend time with God. The busier Jesus was, the more time he spent in prayer. In the middle of a busy schedule, he often withdrew to pray, sometimes spending long hours into the night on his knees (Matt. 14:23; 26:36; Luke 4:42; 5:16; 6:12). In one such instance, Jesus arose before dawn and went off to a "solitary place" to pray (Mark 1:35). Commenting on this verse, Henri Nouwen notes that in the midst of numerous "breathless activities" in which

Jesus healed suffering people, cast out demons, responded to impatient disciples, and preached, he takes a restful breather: "Surrounded by hours of moving we find a moment of quiet stillness. In the heart of much involvement there are words of withdrawal. In the midst of action there is contemplation. And after much togetherness there is solitude. . . . The secret of Jesus' ministry is hidden in that lonely place where he went to pray, early in the morning, long before dawn. In the lonely place Jesus finds the courage to follow God's will and not his own; to speak God's words and not his own; to do God's work and not his own. . . . It is in the lonely place, where Jesus enters into intimacy with the Father, that his ministry is born."[63]

If Jesus pulled away from the hustle and bustle of ministry to pray, how much more do you and I need to do the same?

Serving in ministry while disconnected from the Lord can cause problems. We all know the story of Mary and Martha (Luke 10:38–42) and how Martha was so caught up in her duties as a hostess that she was unable to enjoy fellowship with Jesus. She became angry and resentful toward Mary for deserting her in the kitchen. She even scolded Jesus for not reprimanding her. "Lord, don't you care that my sister has left me to do the work by myself? Tell her to help me!" (v. 40). Trying to serve the Lord while out of fellowship with him can render us vulnerable to anger and resentment.

Mary chose "what is better" (v. 42). Jesus surely would

have rebuked her if she was being lazy; but he didn't, so she wasn't. She was simply choosing fellowship with God over busyness. Throughout the Bible whenever we see Mary, she is always at the feet of Jesus (John 11:32; 12:3). She had a friendship with Christ because she made intimacy with the Savior a priority over her tasks. It seems she was never too busy for Jesus.

Back to Martha. She always seems to get a bad rap whenever this story is told, doesn't she? Are we being fair to Martha? Wasn't she being a good and faithful servant? She had a houseful of hungry fishermen. What was she supposed to do? I ask these questions because those of us involved in worship ministry, especially leaders, face the same dilemma. What are we supposed to do when the demands of ministry prevent us from spending time with the Lord?

I know it's not easy to find time for the Lord. Our schedules are jam-packed; there's always so much to do and not enough time. But I hope you're convinced that the alternative—doing life and ministry disconnected from God—is not an option. After all, what does it profit an artist to gain success or even fame and lose his or her soul by failing to cultivate a vital relationship with God (Luke 9:25)? It is imperative that we make spending time with Jesus a priority and ruthlessly guard those appointments with him.

To my surprise, I discovered that making my quiet time a priority increased my capacity to get things done. The Lord seems to somehow redeem the time we spend with him. I can't explain how that happens. The workload didn't subside, that's for sure. The tyranny of the urgent is always staring us in the face. Maybe I was able to work more efficiently because my soul was in a better place. Or perhaps I was better equipped to face the heavy demands of life because I had spent time at the feet of Jesus. Because my output didn't suffer but actually increased, I became adamant about protecting my quiet times with the Lord. Find a time and place to meet regularly with God, and guard it like a hawk!

Memorizing Scripture

Another spiritual discipline that I heartily recommend is Scripture memorization. Memorizing Scripture plays a significant role in renewing the mind for the purpose of transformation (Rom. 12:2). First Corinthians 14:20 says, "Stop thinking like children. . . . In your thinking be adults." As a young Christian, I quickly realized that God's ways are far from my natural, dysfunctional way of thinking (Isa. 55:8). I remember being discouraged that I couldn't even think like a Christian, let alone act like one.

Then I met an older man who knew large amounts of Scripture by heart. When asked his opinion, he'd always quote a Bible verse that spoke directly to the situation. He wasn't showing off; he was one of the humblest men I've ever met. I remember thinking, *Wouldn't it be great to know that much Scripture from memory so you could instantly recall a passage whenever you needed it?* That's when I decided to start memorizing Scripture.

God's Word has been the biggest change agent in my life. Changing the way I think has changed the way I behave (Ps. 119:11). I concur with Dallas Willard, who writes, "As a pastor, teacher, and counselor I have repeatedly seen the transformation of inner and outer life that comes simply from memorization and meditation upon Scripture. Personally, I would never undertake to pastor a church or guide a program of Christian education that did not involve a continuous program of memorization of the choicest passages of Scripture for people of all ages."[64]

I say with confidence that Scripture memorization will change your life.

Committing Scripture to memory also makes the Bible come to life. While ruminating on a verse I'm memorizing, I often see something in it that I never noticed before. Having the Word of God readily available—treasured in my heart, on the tip of my tongue—has served me well when facing temptation and dealing with the daily challenges of life.

My efforts with this discipline began with the Topical Memory System put out by the Navigators, which is still available today along with a number of online resources. You could also put your favorite Bible verses on note cards or on your phone and memorize those. Scripture memorization involves some work on our part, but it is certainly worth it.

The Daily Dangerous Prayer

Another spiritual discipline, which I alluded to earlier in this book, is what I refer to as my daily dangerous prayer. This is a short, one-line prayer, usually based on a Scripture verse, that I like to pray daily (normally at breakfast) for about a year. It's dangerous because I try to pick a verse that threatens my status quo, a verse that can shake me out of my spiritual complacency and revolutionize my life. Here are some examples.

"Lord, help me to die to self" (John 12:24).

"Lord, I present my body, and the members of my body, to you as instruments of righteousness" (Rom. 6:13).

"Lord, help me to love Jesus more" (John 17:26).

"Father, grant me the kind of obedience that flows out of my love for Jesus" (John 14:21).

"Lord, help me to put the needs of others ahead of my own" (Phil. 2:3–4).

"Lord, have your way with me" (Ps. 139:23–24).

"Lord, help me to do all that I do to your glory today" (Col. 3:23).

"Give me the strength to do all you want me to do" (Phil. 4:13).

People sometimes ask whether it gets monotonous praying the same thing over and over, but it doesn't. Maybe it's because I feel strongly about what I'm praying. If you're going to ask God for the same thing every day, make sure it's something you're passionate about. I've also discovered that the verse might remain the same, but I may apply it in various ways because my needs change over time. So it doesn't feel like I'm praying the same prayer over and over. One year my daily prayer was, "Lord, stretch out your hand and work among us" (Acts 4:30). I prayed that verse on behalf of my family ("Lord, stretch out your hand and work in the lives of my two sons") as well as my friends ("Lord, stretch out your hand and reconcile that marriage, heal that infirmity, save that lost brother"). The prayer took on different forms throughout the year. If praying something for an entire year sounds daunting, shorten the timetable to thirty or forty days. Feel free to modify and adapt this discipline to your situation.

Avoid Legalism

Be sure to avoid legalism when it comes to the spiritual disciplines. Meeting with God in the morning is no more special than meeting with him at night. And if you miss one now and then or experience inconsistencies, don't get down on yourself and withdraw farther from God. Some of you might be in a season of life when the spiritual disciplines are especially difficult. Being a young mom, for example, can be a highly demanding season during which your time is not your own. God understands, so do the best you can. If you can't keep your usual appointment with the Lord, try to find another pocket of time in your day when you can read Scripture and pray. Take advantage of any unexpected moments of solitude that do come your way. You may suddenly find yourself with five or ten minutes of peace and quiet in the middle of a relentlessly busy and noisy day. Consider it a gift from the Lord. Instead of escaping into a video game or some other source of entertainment, relax with God, acknowledge and enjoy his presence. If you're alone in the car, turn off the radio and be with the Lord instead. During seasons of stress that disrupt your normal routine, take advantage of any and every opportunity God provides to be with him.

The Greatest of These Is Still Love

During my days as a youth pastor, a student shared something with me that I found rather troubling. He was sharing about some difficulties at home and said, "I don't know why my dad reads the Bible. It sure doesn't make him a more loving person." The remark caught me off guard because his father was a pillar in our church and had a reputation for being upright and godly. Yet all his son could see was a religious and spiritually disciplined man who was as cold as ice, even cruel at times.

While it's always easy to criticize someone else, that experience forced me to look at my own life. I had to face the truth that I can be just as hypocritical. I can emerge from a deeply meaningful time with the Lord and within ten minutes snap at my wife and kids. Echoing Paul's famous words, if I speak with the tongues of men and of angels and have my quiet time every day but do not have love, I am nothing (1 Cor. 13:1–2).

In John 5:39–47, Jesus denounces the Pharisees for being disciplined in the Scriptures but not having the love of God in their hearts. They knew their Hebrew Bible inside out, yet they never saw Jesus in them. They knew great amounts of Scripture from memory and still missed the point of it all. Don't let this happen to you. When you read the Bible, think about how you can apply it to your life. Ezra was a man who set his heart not only to study God's Word but also to live according to God's Word (Ezra 7:10). Spiritual transformation doesn't happen when we fill our heads with all sorts of knowledge. It happens when we apply what we read to our lives. Read the Bible with every intention of doing what it says and it'll change your behavior.

The true mark of a Christian is not how disciplined you are or how much Bible knowledge you attain but how loving you are. If spending time with God doesn't make you a more loving person, you're not spending time with the God of the Bible. Our God is a loving God. Jesus told his disciples to follow his example by loving others. "A new command I give you: Love one another. As I have loved you, so you must love one another. By this everyone will know that you are my disciples, if you love one another" (John 13:34–35). This wasn't really a new commandment for them, any more than it is for us. They had heard it all before, and so have we. That's the problem—we've heard it a lot. But hearing it does not make us more loving people. We need to make the effort to love others.

Paul tells us to pursue love (1 Cor. 14:1). The best way to do that is to dwell deeply in God's love. Dallas Willard explains that as we catch God's love and dwell in it, we ourselves become more loving, patient, and kind; as we become permeated with the love of Christ, doing what Jesus said and did becomes a natural expression of who we are in Christ.[65] Dwelling in God's love means that if one of your kids interrupts your quiet time, you don't lash out in anger or frustration. Being with your heavenly Father reminds you to respond with love and patience. Dwelling in God's love should make us more loving as people.

Don't fall into the trap of becoming more disciplined and less loving. "Let us not love with words or speech but with actions and in truth" (1 John 3:18). When you meet with the Lord, soak in all the unconditional love he has for you and keep coming back to it throughout your day so you can continue to dwell in his love. May all you do, in life and in ministry, be done in love (1 Cor. 16:14). In the final analysis, the heart of a God-honoring artist overflows with love for Jesus, for others, for the things that stir God's heart, and for the blessed gifts of art, creativity, and beauty.

Follow-Up Questions for Group Discussion

1. Do you agree or disagree with the stereotype that portrays artists as undisciplined? Why or why not?
2. What do you think about the ministry principle presented in this chapter—that your ministry is the product of your relationship with Christ? Do you believe that's true? Why or why not?
3. What disciplines or practices enable you to nurture a vital, healthy relationship with the Lord?
4. What challenges do people face in establishing a regular quiet time, and what suggestions do you have for overcoming those challenges?

5. What practices have you found helpful when reading the Bible?

6. What practices do you find helpful for prayer?

7. Do you think journaling or using a prayer list is a good idea? Why or why not?

8. Do you have any advice for those just starting to establish a routine for private devotions?

9. Do you have any other suggestions for interjecting variety or life into your times with God?

PERSONAL ACTION STEPS

1. Identify a spiritual discipline or practice that you would like to incorporate more regularly into your schedule and decide how you can make that happen.

2. If you don't have a regular quiet time, select a time and place for your meeting times with the Lord.

3. Early church leaders were so devoted to prayer and God's Word that they adamantly protected those two priorities in their schedules. In Acts 6 they even changed the serving structure of their church to ensure that the leaders had more time for prayer and God's Word. Determine whether there are any radical changes you need to make to ensure that you commune regularly with God.

4. Decide which Scripture verses you would like to memorize and choose someone to whom you can be accountable in following through with that commitment.

5. Write down a one-line prayer request, your daily dangerous prayer, that you feel led to pray every day for the next year.

NOTES

1. Rudolf and Margot Wittkower, *Born under Saturn: The Character and Conduct of Artists; A Documented History from Antiquity to the French Revolution* (New York: Norton, 1963), 102.
2. Ibid.
3. Ibid.
4. Ibid.
5. Ibid.
6. Ken Gire, *Windows of the Soul: Experiencing God in New Ways* (Grand Rapids: Zondervan, 1996), 20.
7. Frank E. Gaebelein, *The Christian, the Arts, and Truth: Regaining the Vision of Greatness* (Portland: Multnomah, 1985), 124.
8. Francis A. Schaeffer, *Art and the Bible* (Downers Grove: InterVarsity, 1973), 12.
9. Patrick Kavanaugh, *The Spiritual Lives of Great Composers* (Nashville: Sparrow, 1992), 6.
10. Charlie Peacock, "The Nine Pursuits of the True Artist," Cross Rhythms, August 1, 1997, accessed July 14, 2020, *https://www.crossrhythms.co.uk/articles/music/Charlie_Peacock_UK_singersongwriter_returns_to_Greenbelt/32536/p2/.*
11. Zac Hicks, *The Worship Pastor: A Call to Ministry for Worship Leaders and Teams* (Grand Rapids: Zondervan, 2016), 22.
12. Barbara Nicolosi, "The Artist: What Exactly Is an Artist, and How Do We Shepherd Them?" in *For the Beauty of the Church*, ed. W. David O. Taylor (Grand Rapids: Baker, 2010), 904, Kindle.
13. John Wooden, *They Call Me Coach* (Waco: Word, 1972), 64.

14. N. T. Wright, *After You Believe: Why Christian Character Matters* (New York: HarperCollins, 2010), 27.
15. David Jeremiah, *Turning toward Integrity: Face Life's Challenges with God's Strength and New Resolve* (Colorado Springs: Victor, 1993), 7.
16. C. S. Lewis, *The Screwtape Letters* (New York: Bantam, 1982), 41.
17. Patrick Kavanaugh, *Spiritual Moments with the Great Composers: Daily Devotions from the Lives of Favorite Composers and Hymn Writers* (Grand Rapids: Zondervan, 1995), 80.
18. C. S. Lewis, *Mere Christianity* (New York: Simon and Schuster, 1996), 110.
19. Richard Foster, *Celebration of Discipline: The Path to Spiritual Growth* (San Francisco: Harper and Row, 1978), 130.
20. C. H. Spurgeon, *The Treasury of David*, vol. 2 (McLean: MacDonald, n.d.), 144–45.
21. Thomas à Kempis, *The Imitation of Christ*, ed. Paul M. Bechtel (Chicago: Moody, 1980), 180.
22. Frederick Buechner, *Wishful Thinking: A Theological ABC* (San Francisco: Harper and Row, 1973), 95.
23. For more information on what it means to bring God your best worship, see chapter 6 of my book *Worship on Earth as It Is in Heaven: Exploring Worship as a Spiritual Discipline.*
24. Philip Yancey, *Open Windows* (Westchester: Crossway, 1982), 211.
25. Anthony E. Kemp, *The Musical Temperament: Psychology and Personality of Musicians* (Oxford: Oxford Univ. Press, 1996), 66.
26. Howard Gardner, *Creating Minds: An Anatomy of Creativity* (New York: Basic, 1993), 195–96.
27. Spiritual gifts are listed in three passages: Rom. 12:6–8; 1 Cor. 12:8–10, 28–30; Eph. 4:11.
28. For a more thorough treatment of resolving relational conflict, see chapter 4 of my book *Thriving as an Artist in the Church: Hope and Help for You and Your Ministry Team.*

29. Brennan Manning, *Abba's Child: The Cry of the Heart for Intimate Belonging* (Colorado Springs: NavPress, 1994), 22–23.
30. Ibid., 19.
31. Willem A. VanGemeren, ed., *New International Dictionary of Old Testament Theology and Exegesis*, vol. 2 (Grand Rapids: Zondervan, 1997), 167–68.
32. For further discussion on the topic of receiving God's love, see my book *The Worshiping Artist: Equipping You and Your Ministry Team to Lead Others in Worship*, 145–47.
33. Mary Soames, *Winston Churchill: His Life as a Painter* (Boston: Houghton Mifflin, 1990), 143.
34. Franky Schaeffer, *Addicted to Mediocrity: Twentieth-Century Christians and the Arts* (Westchester: Crossway, 1981), 45–46.
35. Ibid., 62.
36. Georg Solti, *Memoirs* (New York: Alfred A. Knopf, 1997), 204.
37. Peggy Noonan, *Simply Speaking: How to Communicate Your Ideas with Style, Substance, and Clarity* (New York: HarperCollins, 1998), 8.
38. Judith Mackrell, "Marvelous Mark Morris," in "Ballet: From Ritual to Romance," special issue, *BBC Music* (1996), 64.
39. Henri Nouwen, *Reaching Out: The Three Movements of the Spiritual Life* (New York: Doubleday, 1975), 70.
40. Dante Alighieri, *Divine Comedy: Purgatorio*, canto 14, trans. John Ciardi (New York: Random House, 1996), 148.
41. Gordon MacDonald, *The Life God Blesses: Weathering the Storms of Life That Threaten the Soul* (Nashville: Nelson, 1994), 143.
42. Jane Stuart Smith and Betty Carlson, *The Gift of Music: Great Composers and Their Influence* (Wheaton: Crossway, 1995), 164.
43. Rudolf and Margot Wittkower, *Born under Saturn: The Character and Conduct of Artists: A Documented History from Antiquity to the French Revolution* (New York: Norton, 1963), 74.

44. Jimmy Webb, *Tunesmith: Inside the Art of Songwriting* (New York: Hyperion, 1998), 370.
45. Richard Foster, *Celebration of Discipline: The Path to Spiritual Growth* (San Francisco: Harper and Row, 1978), 102.
46. John Piper, *Desiring God: Meditations of a Christian Hedonist* (Sisters: Multnomah, 1986), 76.
47. William Temple, *Readings in St. John's Gospel*, vol. 1 (London: Macmillan, 1939), 68.
48. C. S. Lewis, *Reflections on the Psalms* (New York: Harcourt Brace, 1958), 94.
49. Rainer Maria Rilke, *Letters to a Young Poet* (San Rafael: New World Library, 1992), 64–65.
50. Cornelius Plantinga Jr., *Not the Way It's Supposed to Be: A Breviary of Sin* (Grand Rapids: Eerdmans, 1995), 135.
51. For further discussion on accountability, see chapter 8 of my book *The Worshiping Artist: Equipping You and Your Ministry Team to Lead Others in Worship.*
52. C. S. Lewis, *Mere Christianity* (New York: Simon and Schuster, 1996), 92.
53. William Gurnall, *The Christian in Complete Armour*, abr. Ruthanne Garlock (Edinburgh: Banner of Trust, 1986), 197.
54. Jerry Bridges, *The Pursuit of Holiness* (Colorado Springs: NavPress, 1978), 78.
55. *Julian of Norwich: Showings*, ed. Edmund Colledge and James Walsh (New York: Paulist Press, 1978), 245.
56. Anthony E. Kemp, *The Musical Temperament: Psychology and Personality of Musicians* (Oxford: Oxford Univ. Press, 1996), 25.
57. David Ewen, *The Complete Book of Classical Music* (Englewood Cliffs: Prentice Hall, 1965), 142.
58. Jack Deere, *Surprised by the Voice of God: How God Speaks Today through Prophecies, Dreams, and Visions* (Grand Rapids: Zondervan, 1996), 331.
59. Ibid.

60. J. I. Packer, *Knowing God* (Downers Grove: InterVarsity, 1973), 29.
61. Henry T. Blackaby and Claude V. King, *Experiencing God: How to Live the Full Adventure of Knowing and Doing the Will of God* (Nashville: Broadman and Holman, 1994), 45.
62. J. Oswald Sanders, *Spiritual Leadership* (Chicago: Moody, 1967), 123.
63. Henri Nouwen, *Out of Solitude: Three Meditations on the Christian Life* (Notre Dame: Ave Maria, 1995), 13–14.
64. Dallas Willard, *Spirit of the Disciplines: Understanding How God Changes Lives* (San Francisco: HarperCollins, 1988), 150.
65. Dallas Willard, *The Divine Conspiracy: Rediscovering Our Hidden Life in God* (San Francisco: HarperCollins, 1998), 183.